LINE GAMES

An In-Depth Study of Single-Note Lines for Guitar

by Randy Vincent

Music Engraving - Chuck Gee
Cover Design - Attila Nagy
Cover Mosaic Art - Sueann Bettison Sher

ISBN 1-883217-74-1

Table Of Contents

Introduction

Unlike my previous jazz guitar chord voicings books (*Jazz Guitar Voicings Vol. 1: The Drop 2 Book* and *Three-Note Voicings and Beyond*, both available from Sher Music Co.), this book is a collection of things to practice on the guitar that will help you develop the vocabulary of jazz improvisation while simultaneously developing and maintaining single-note technique. I have included many lines and phrases transcribed from the recordings of several master guitarists (and occasionally saxophonists, trumpeters, and pianists as well) to demonstrate the validity of the concepts behind the exercises given.

The topics roughly follow concepts in the same order as I became aware of them in my own development, but not always. For example, the triad-pair concept in chapter 3 came much later in my own playing, while the pluralities concept from chapter 4 came very early. Of course they don't really happen one after another but are very overlapping.

To use this book you should have some basic knowledge of standard music notation and the ability to find notes anywhere on the guitar. When strings and fingerings are shown, the strings are the numbers inside small circles (above the staff), while the fingers are numbers without circles (below the staff). It's standard guitar fingering, with 1 being the index finger, 2 the middle, 3 the ring, and 4 the "pinky". When there's a straight line between repeated finger numbers, that finger slides along the string it's on to the next note. When there's a bracket below repeated finger numbers, that finger rolls to an adjacent string on the same fret to play the next note. If the roll is to a higher pitched string the roll starts on the finger tip and rolls over to the side of the finger. If the roll is to a lower pitched string the roll starts on the side of the finger and rolls over to the finger tip. Occasionally the notes on the same fret will be on non-adjacent strings, but the technique will be the same. All the fingerings are suggestions only, so if something else works better for you, by all means feel free.

There will be a follow-up volume that will use the the concept of melodic cells to address various fast moving changes, such as quick cycles, turnarounds, Coltrane changes, etc. It will also address playing "outside" of the changes and "free" improvisation as well. The epilogue to this book will introduce these topics with a few examples to get you started.

About the Author

Randy Vincent has had a long and illustrious career in jazz. He has performed, toured and/or recorded with Dizzy Gillespie, Joe Henderson, Bobby Hutcherson, Bebop And Beyond, The Turtle Island String Quartet, Leny Andrade, Denise Donatelli and many others.

Randy has taught jazz guitar at Sonoma State University since 1981 and has conducted clinics throughout the US and overseas. Some of his more well-known former students include Julian Lage, Dave MacNab, Chris Pimentel, and Liberty Ellmen. He currently teaches at Sonoma State University and privately.

He is the author of two previous Sher Music Co. books, "Jazz Guitar Voicings, Vol.1 - The Drop 2 Book," and "Three-Note Voicings and Beyond," both of which have received wide critical acclaim.

He has performed at numerous jazz festivals including the Monterey Jazz Festival and Dizzy Gillespie's 75th birthday celebration at the Hollywood Bowl, as well as performing regularly with the Santa Rosa Symphony's Pops Concerts.

A selected discography of Randy's recordings:

Randy Vincent - "Nisha's Dream" and "Mirror Image"
Bobby Hutcherson - "Ambos Mundos"
Bebop And Beyond - "Bebop And Beyond Plays Dizzy Gillespie" (featuring Dizzy)
and "Bebop And Beyond Plays Thelonious Monk" (featuring Joe Henderson)
Stephanie Ozer - "O Comeco" (featuring Leny Andrade)
Larry Baskett Trio - "Chalice" and "Poor Boy Blue"
Mel Graves - "Emotion In Motion"
Turtle Island String Quartet - "Spider Dreams"
Peter Welker - "Para Peachy" and "We'll Be Together Again"
Welker/Oster Jazz Alliance - "Shining Hour" and "Detour Ahead"
Vern Thompson - "Passions Of The Heart", "Sea Of Dreams" and "Convergence"
(featuring Bob Sheppard, Akira Tana, Tony Dumas and Billy Childs)
Mike Vax Big Band - "Alternate Route"
Dave Eshelman's Garden Big Band - "Milagro's Journey"
Steve Puleo - "Smile"
Deborah Winters - "Lovers After All"

Chapter 1 - Basic Hexatonic Scales for Jazz Improvisation

The Types of Basic Hexatonic Scales

Definition of hexatonic scales

This chapter is primarily about what I'm calling "basic hexatonic scales." Strictly speaking any pitch-collection consisting of six different notes can be called a hexatonic scale. As we'll see in Chapter 3, the term is often used to refer to modern-sounding scales created by combining two major or two minor triads (usually a whole step apart). In this chapter, however, we'll be looking at how to create and use the more traditional-sounding (swing and bebop) hexatonic scales.

For example, the Cmaj7-Ami7 hexatonic shown below (ex.1-A) contains the same six notes as the traditional G "Scottish hexatonic scale" (ex.1-B) and can be analyzed as the triad-pair of G major and A minor (ex.1-C), but generally isn't broken up that way in this chapter. Instead, you'll see that it's more useful to think of it as composed of three two-note "cells" (ex.1-D) that can be manipulated in various ways to create many great-sounding lines.

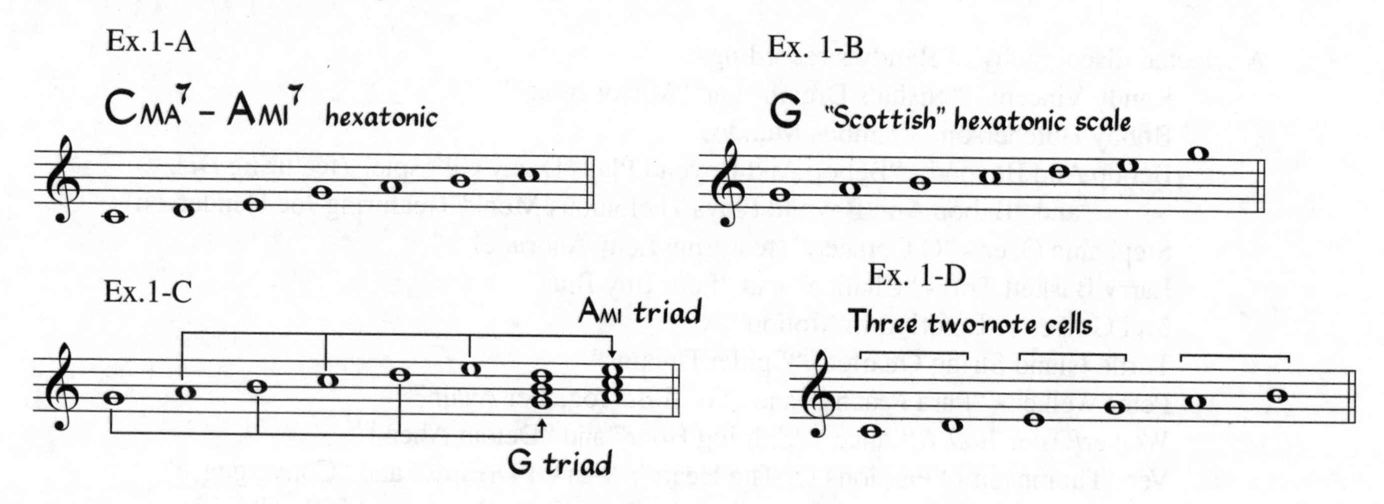

The types of hexatonics examined in this chapter will primarily be:

First, the maj7 (root, 2nd, 3rd, 5th, 6th, and maj7th of major) and its relative minor (root, 2nd, mi3rd, 4th, 5th, and mi7th), as in Ex. 1-A above. This scale is applied to maj7, mi7, and 7sus chords.

Secondly, the mi-maj7 (root, 2nd, mi3rd, 5th, 6th, and maj7th), also sometimes called "melodic minor hexatonic," which is applied to maj7#5, mi-maj7, mi7b5, 7susb9, and 7alt chords.

Some actual examples of hexatonic improvisation on mi7 chords

Play ex.1-1, taken from an early recording by Joe Pass.

This is a clear example of using a six-note, or *hexatonic* scale to create a line over a mi7 chord. If you're thinking it's just a melody he heard derived from Ab dorian, well, that may be true in that I never heard or read Joe himself refer to hexatonic scales (or dorian mode either), but he sure used them a lot and included many examples in his own books. As evidence play ex. 1-2 and ex.1-3 from the same recording. Pure hexatonic.

Of course hexatonics are used by many other players as well. For instance listen to ex.1-4 from a Pat Martino recording. Then check out ex.1-5 through ex.1-8 (on the next page), all from Wes Montgomery.

Ex.1-8

In ex.1-8 Wes has spread the hexatonic out into a Gmi11 arpeggio. Ex.1-9 shows the basic Gmi7 hexatonic scale that Wes is using in ex.1-8, while ex.1-10 shows it as an arpeggio, the way Wes actually played it.

Ex.1-9

Ex.1-10

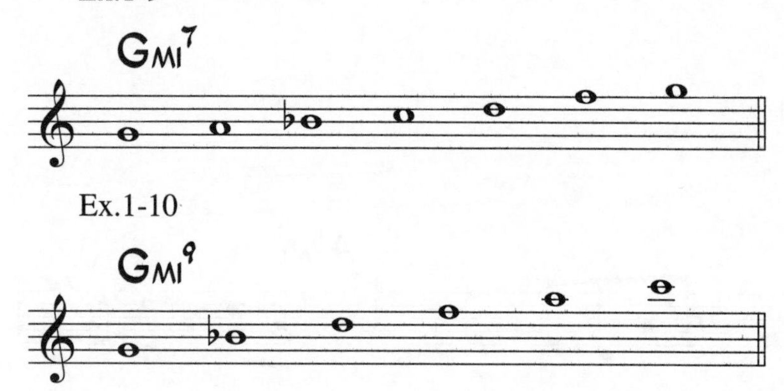

Hexatonic scale for maj7 chords

Ex.1-11 shows an arpeggio for a Bbmaj9 chord with a 13th added. Bb is the relative major of G minor, and this arpeggio contains the same notes as the Gmi11 arpeggio. From this we can derive a Bb major hexatonic scale, shown in ex.1-12. It has the same notes as the Gmi7 hexatonic scale shown in ex.1-9.

Ex.1-11

Ex.1-12

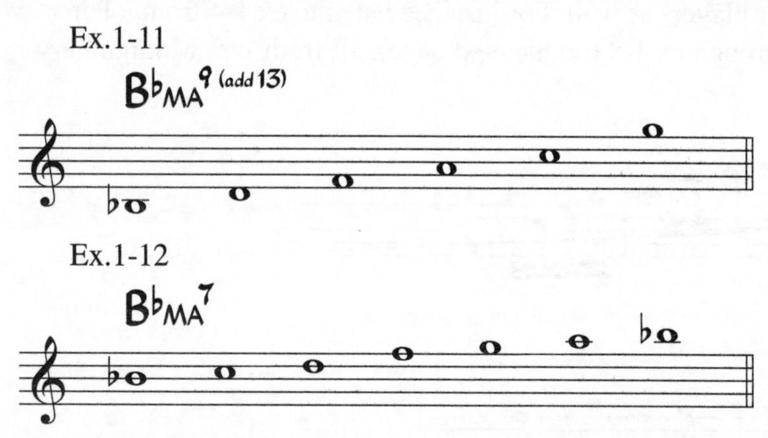

The major hexatonic scale can be thought of in different ways. I originally conceived of it as a major scale with the potentially dangerous 4th step removed, making improvisation easier on major chords. Joe Diorio viewed it as a relative minor pentatonic with an added 9th. My former student Julian Lage reports that saxophonist Dayna Stephens thinks of mixing a maj7 arpeggio with a major pentatonic scale.

Some actual examples of hexatonic improv on maj7 chords

Play ex.1-13 and ex.1-14. These are from Joe Pass recordings showing him using the major hexatonic scale to create lines over maj7 chords.

Ex.1-13

Ex.1-14

Now play ex.1-15 from Pat Martino.

Also try ex.1-16 from Wes Montgomery.

Some actual examples of hexatonic improv on altered dominant chords

Wes also provides us with ex.1-17 showing a hexatonic line over an altered dominant chord (if you're unclear about what altered chords are, check out *The Jazz Theory Book* by Mark Levine from Sher Music Co.). Our previous Maj13-relative mi11 hexatonic scale does not really fit the altered sound, so Wes shows us a new combination that really does fit.

Play ex.1-18 from Joe Pass. This is a classic II-V-I line that uses the mi7 hexatonic on the II chord and the altered dominant hexatonic on the V chord.

Ex.1-19 and ex.1-20 are from Joe Pass recordings showing altered hexatonics resolving to minor chords.

Ex.1-19

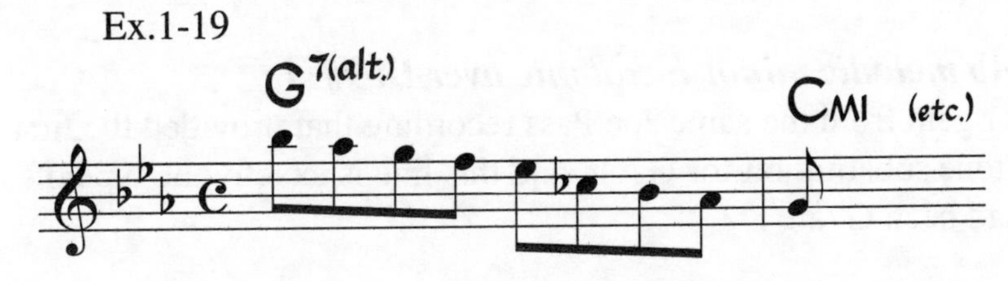

Ex.1-20

The altered hexatonic and the melodic minor hexatonic

Ex.1-21 shows the basic G7alt hexatonic scale. It has the b9 and #9, the b4th functions as the major 3rd, and there's a b13th and the b7th.

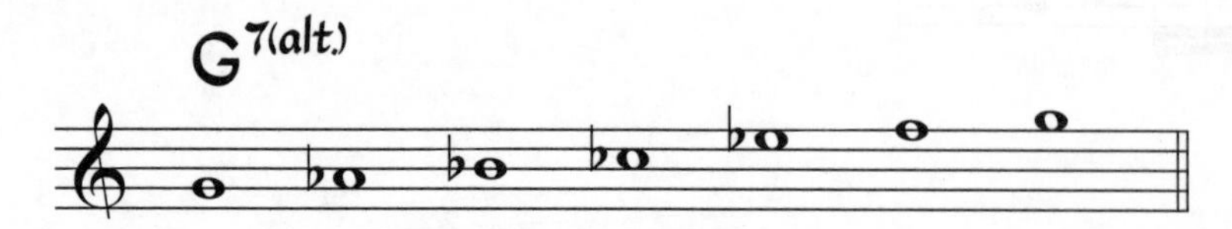

It contains the same notes as ex.1-22 below, which we could call Ab melodic minor hexatonic. It's the same as an Ab major hexatonic with a lowered 3rd. It fits Abmi-maj7 as well as Abmi6, Abmi6/9, etc.

Other uses for melodic minor hexatonics

Ex.1-23 shows the Ab melodic minor hexatonic spread out as an arpeggio, placing F on the bottom and spelling out Fm11b5 with a natural 9.

Next I've added a Db note in parenthesis under the arpeggio, converting it into Db13#11 with a natural 9 (ex.1-24). The parenthesis indicates that we won't actually use that note in our hexatonic lines, but the lines still work over that chord.

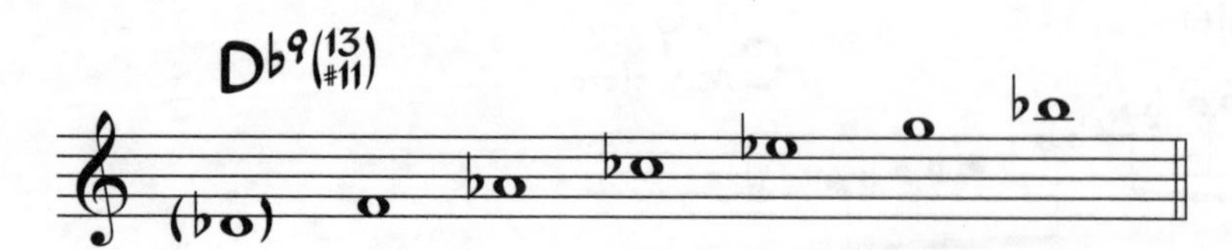

An actual example of Ab melodic minor hexatonic over Db9#11

Play ex.1-25 (on the following page), another gem from the same Joe Pass recording that provided the first three examples. The Db9#11 is actually a tritone substitution for G7alt, and this line is exactly the type of line that Joe would likely play if the chord had been G7alt.

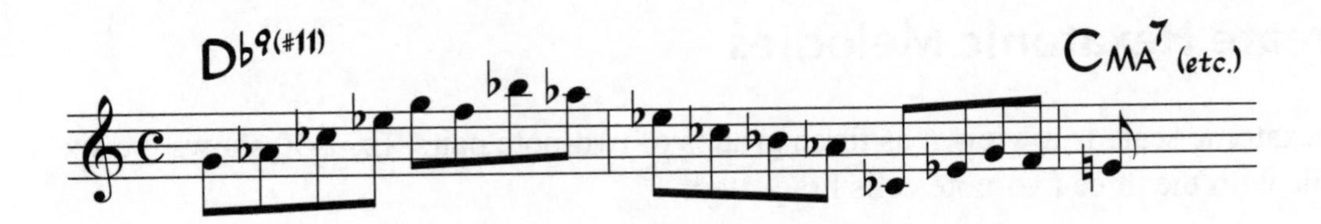

The 13susb9 chord

Play ex.1-26. This G13susb9 hexatonic scale actually has the same notes as the F melodic minor hexatonic scale. When used as a dominant in C major, it's like borrowing the altered V chord from the relative minor (E7alt in A minor). As the upcoming examples demonstrate, this sound can be used on the straight dom7 chord.

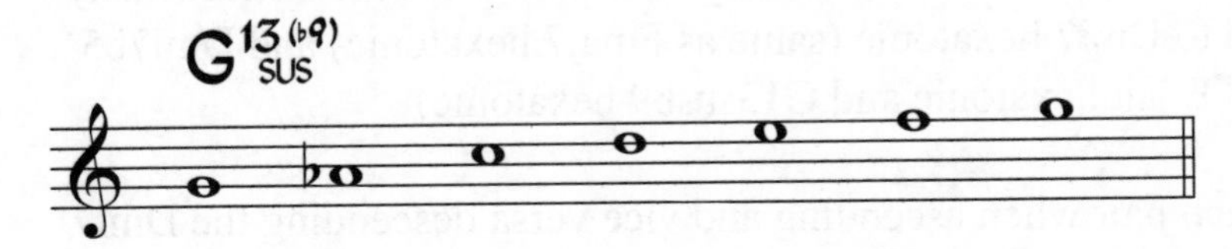

Actual examples of 13susb9 hexatonics

Joe Pass again provides ex.1-27 through 1-29. Ex.1-27 and ex.1-28 are pure hexatonic using the Fmaj13-Dmi11 hexatonic over the Dmi7 and the G13susb9 (F melodic minor) hexatonic over the G7.

Ex.1-27

Ex.1-28

Ex.1-29 has an added chromatic passing tone during the II chord, a subject for a future chapter.

A System to Create Hexatonic Melodies

One way to look at a hexatonic scale is to view it as three groups of two-note pairs. Ex.1-30 shows the six notes of Dmi7 hexatonic with the three two-note cells bracketed.

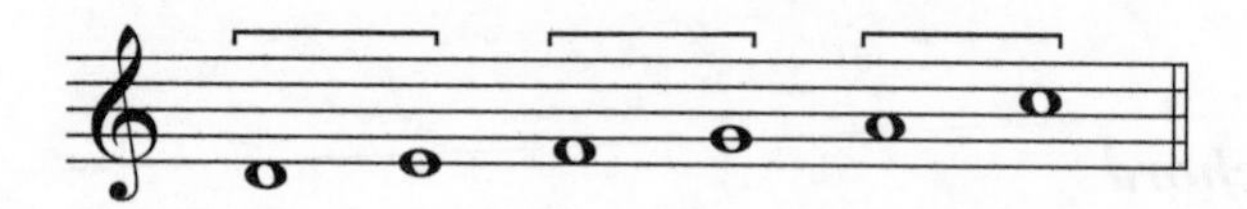

In most of the non-arpeggio examples shown above, when one of the notes from a cell appears the other note of that cell occurs before the line moves elsewhere. The following examples will demonstrate many combinations that follow that "rule" applied to Dmi7 hexatonic (same as Fmaj7 hexatonic) and Dmi7b5 hexatonic (same as Fmi-maj7 hexatonic and E7alt hexatonic and G13susb9 hexatonic).

Ex.1-31 reverses the order of the notes in each pair when ascending and vice versa descending the Dmi7 hexatonic scale. Ex.1-32 shows the same thing applied to the Dmi7b5 hexatonic scale.

In ex.1-33 we begin with an ascending pair, then reverse every other time ascending and descending the Dmi7 hexatonic scale. Ex.1-34 shows the same thing applied to the Dmi7b5 hexatonic scale.

In ex.1-35 we begin with a descending pair, then reverse every other time ascending and descending the Dmi7 hexatonic scale. Ex.1-36 shows the same thing applied to the Dmi7b5 hexatonic scale.

Ex.1-36

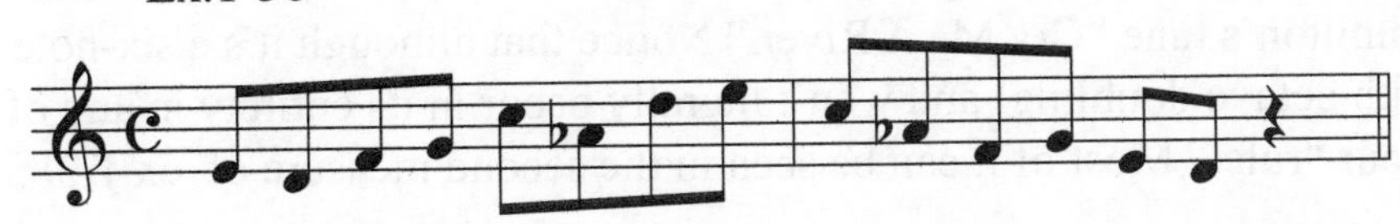

In ex.1-37 we skip cells and then return to them before skipping again. This still complies with the "rule" above, using the Dmi7 hexatonic scale. Ex.1-38 shows the same thing applied to the Dmi7b5 hexatonic scale.

Ex.1-37

Ex.1-38

Ex.1-39 combines cell skipping with reversing the direction of every other pair ascending and descending the Dmi7 hexatonic scale. Ex.1-40 shows the same thing applied to the Dmi7b5 hexatonic scale.

Ex.1-39

Ex.1-40

Deriving two famous quotes from the "rule"

Play ex.1-41, a famous six-note quote that was used frequently in the Joe Pass examples above. It closely resembles the opening melodic phrase from the Fats Waller tune "Honeysuckle Rose." Notice that it occurred in the second measure of ex.1-39.

Now play ex.1-42, a famous six-note quote frequently used by most jazz musicians. It closely resembles the opening melodic phrase from Arthur Hamilton's tune "Cry Me A River." Notice that although it's a six-note phrase, it only uses four pitches (two with octave doubling) and won't literally occur in its entirety in any of the above examples, but it still follows our "rule." Most of it can be seen in the second measure of ex.1-38.

The "Honeysuckle Rose" phrase is derived from the maj7-relative mi7 hexatonic scale, while the "Cry Me A River" phrase was derived from the mi-maj7-relative mi7b5 hexatonic scale. Let's see what happens if we reverse those modal qualities. Ex.1-43 shows the "Honeysuckle Rose" phrase converted to melodic minor, and ex.1-44 shows the "Cry Me A River" phrase converted to major, yielding two more useful melodic fragments (they're still hexatonic and still follow the "rule").

Ex.1-43

Ex.1-44

Positional Hexatonic Scale Fingerings

Now we need to develop some fingerings and basic exercises to give us access to hexatonic fluency all over the guitar. Let's start with some basic across-the-fingerboard positional fingerings that will give us the ability to play lines without a lot of difficult position shifts or finger stretches (we'll get to long moving patterns with lots of shifting later).

The Cmaj7-Ami7 hexatonic scale fingering and exercises in the second position

Look at ex.1-45, a practical fingerboard pattern for playing the Cmaj7-Ami7 hexatonic scale in the second position. Some alternate fingerings are given on the sixth, second and first strings which may make some of the exercises easier to play.

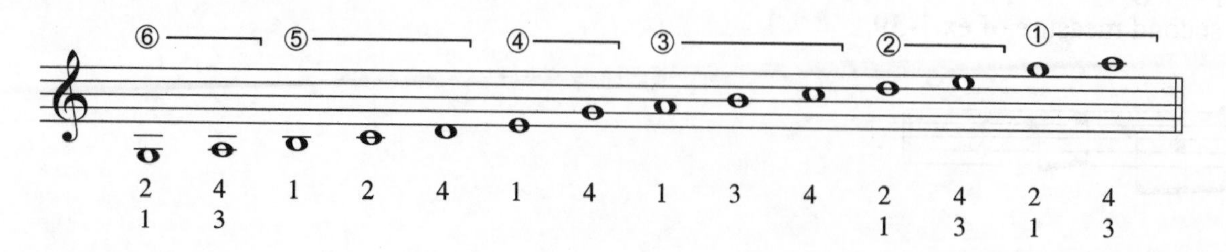

Ex.1-46 shows a way to play the scale up and down while still following the "rule." In addition you should create full-range versions in this key of examples 1-31, 1-33, 1-35, 1-37 and 1-39. I know that's a lot of homework for you, but I don't want to deprive you of the pleasure of working them out yourself by writing them all out for you (I worked them out for myself and the pleasure was really good).

Ex.1-47 is an example of a practice "loop" that can be repeated many times to develop melodic fluency in this fingering pattern. This loop and all the Cmaj7-Ami7 exercises can be played over Emi7 when it's a III chord (in the key of C major), Cmaj7(9,13), Ami7(9,11), Fmaj13#11, and D13sus!

The Cmi-maj7 hexatonic scale fingering and exercises in the second and third positions

Ex.1-48 shows a practical fingerboard pattern for playing the Cmi-maj7 hexatonic scale in the second position, including some alternate fingerings.

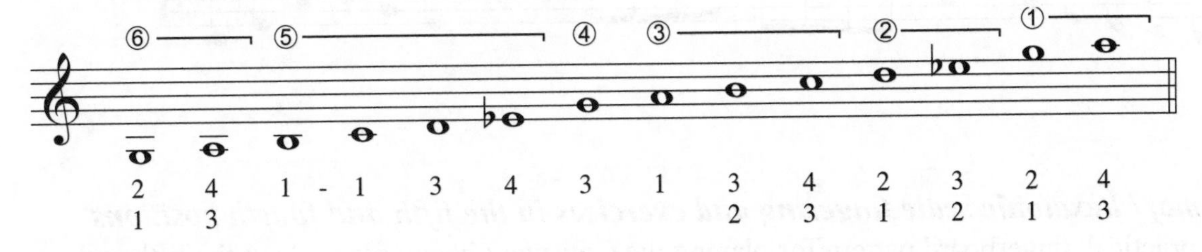

Ex.1-49 shows a way to play the scale up and down while still following the "rule." In addition you should create full-range versions in this key of examples 1-32, 1-34, 1-36, 1-38 and 1-40.

Ex.1-50 is a practice loop based on the same melodic shapes as ex.1-47, but changed to melodic minor. This loop and all the Cmi-maj7 exercises can be played over Ebmaj7#5, Cmi-maj7(9,13), Ami7b5(9,11), F13#11, D13susb9 and B7alt.

The Cmaj7-Ami7 hexatonic scale fingering and exercises in the fifth and fourth positions

Ex.1-51 shows a practical fingerboard pattern for playing the Cmaj7-Ami7 hexatonic scale in the fifth and fourth positions.

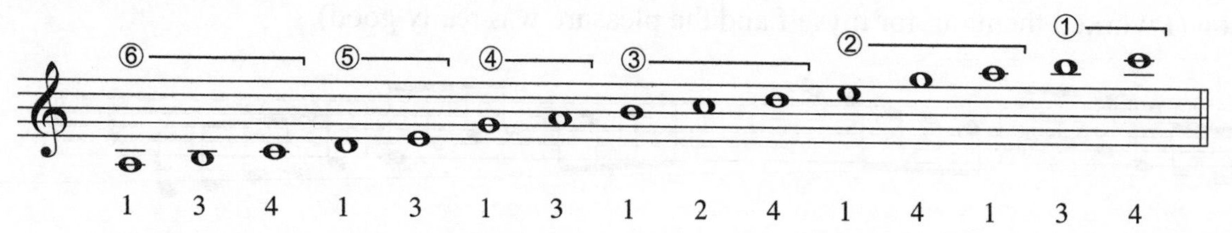

Ex.1-52 shows a way to play the scale up and down while still following the "rule." In addition you should create full-range versions in this key of examples 1-31, 1-33, 1-35, 1-37 and 1-39.

Ex.1-53 is a practice loop for this fingerboard pattern that works on all the same chords mentioned in ex.1-47.

The Cmi-maj7 hexatonic scale fingering and exercises in the fifth and fourth positions

Ex.1-54 shows a practical fingerboard pattern for playing the Cmi-maj7 hexatonic scale in the fifth and fourth positions.

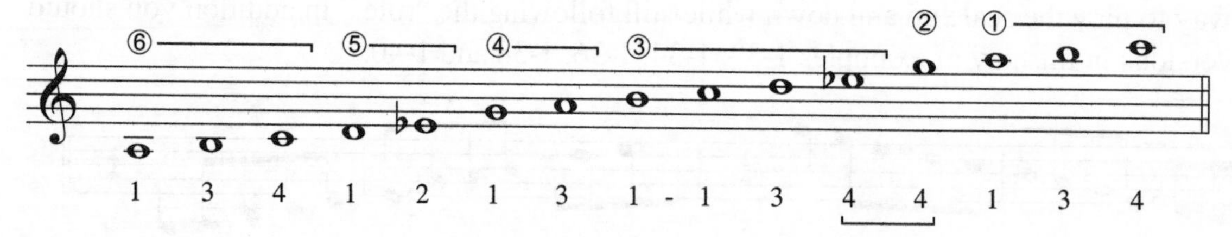

Ex.1-55 shows a way to play the scale up and down while still following the "rule." In addition you should create full-range versions in this key of examples 1-32, 1-34, 1-36, 1-38 and 1-40.

Ex.1-56 is a practice loop for this fingerboard pattern that works on all the same chords mentioned in ex.1-50.

The Cmaj7-Ami7 hexatonic scale fingering and exercises in the seventh position

Ex.1-57 shows a practical fingerboard pattern for playing the Cmaj7-Ami7 hexatonic scale in the seventh position.

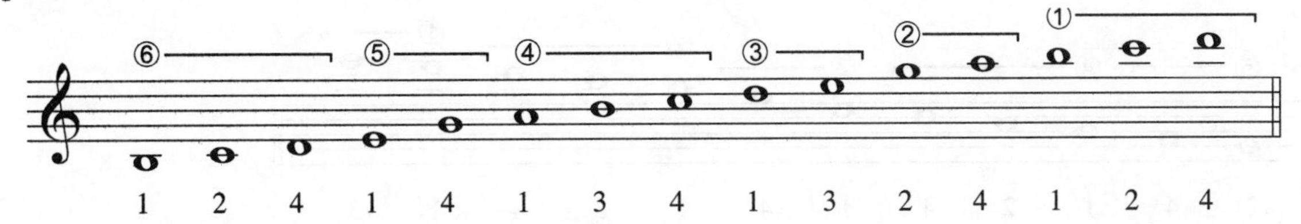

Ex.1-58 shows a way to play the scale up and down while still following the "rule." In addition you should create full-range versions in this key of examples 1-31, 1-33, 1-35, 1-37 and 1-39.

Ex.1-59 is a practice loop for this fingerboard pattern that works on all the same chords mentioned in ex.1-47.

The Cmi-maj7 hexatonic scale fingering and exercises in the seventh position

Ex.1-60 shows a practical fingerboard pattern for playing the Cmi-maj7 hexatonic scale in the seventh position.

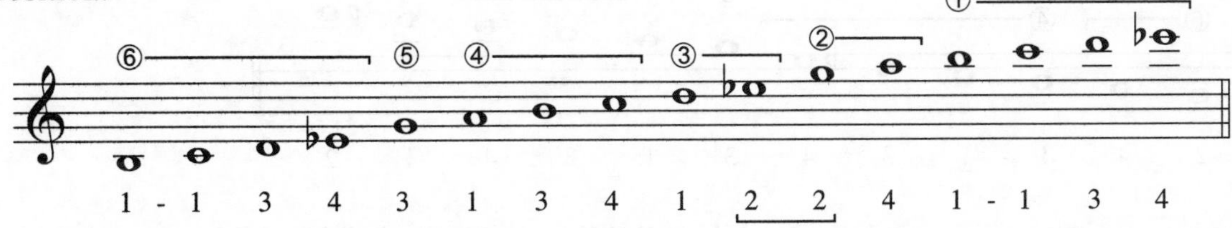

Ex.1-61 shows a way to play the scale up and down while still following the "rule." In addition you should create full-range versions in this key of examples 1-32, 1-34, 1-36, 1-38 and 1-40.

Ex.1-62 is a practice loop for this fingerboard pattern that works on all the same chords mentioned in ex.1-50.

The Cmaj7-Ami7 hexatonic scale fingering and exercises in the tenth and ninth positions

Ex.1-63 shows a practical fingerboard pattern for playing the Cmaj7-Ami7 hexatonic scale in the tenth and ninth positions.

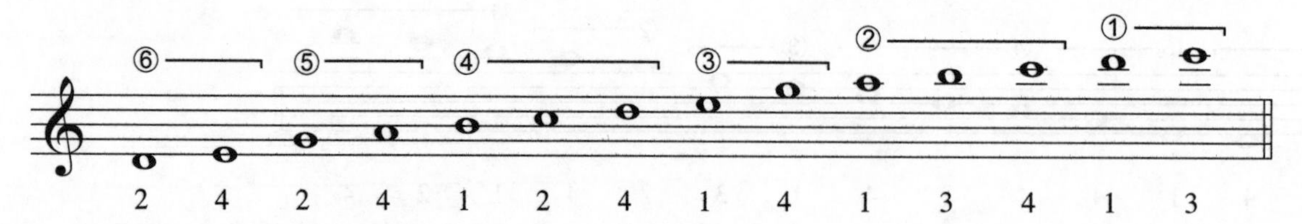

Ex.1-64 shows a way to play the scale up and down while still following the "rule." In addition you should create full-range versions in this key of examples 1-31, 1-33, 1-35, 1-37 and 1-39.

Ex.1-65 is a practice loop for this fingerboard pattern that works on all the same chords mentioned in ex.1-47.

The Cmi-maj7 hexatonic scale fingering and exercises in the tenth and ninth positions

Ex.1-66 shows a practical fingerboard pattern for playing the Cmi-maj7 hexatonic scale in the tenth and ninth positions.

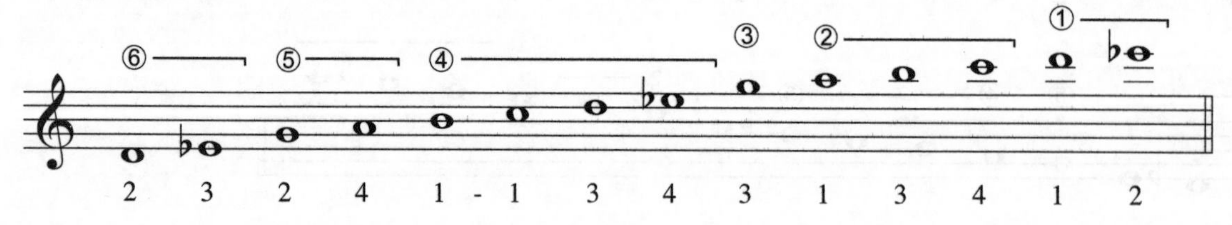

Ex.1-67 shows a way to play the scale up and down while still following the "rule." In addition you should create full-range versions in this key of examples 1-32, 1-34, 1-36, 1-38 and 1-40.

Ex.1-68 is a practice loop for this fingerboard pattern that works on all the same chords mentioned in ex.1-50.

The Cmaj7-Ami7 hexatonic scale fingering and exercises in the twelfth position

Ex.1-69 shows a practical fingerboard pattern for playing the Cmaj7-Ami7 hexatonic scale in the twelfth position.

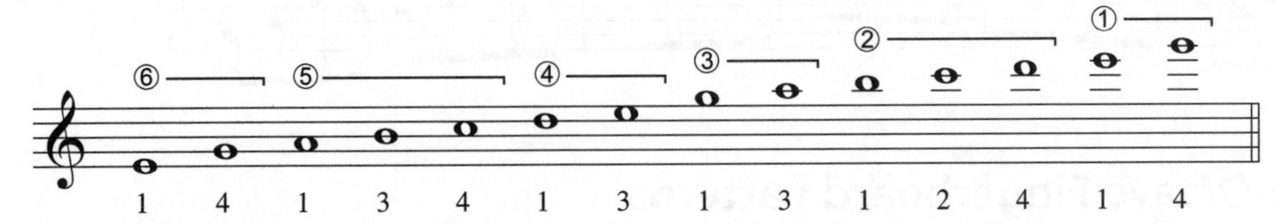

Ex.1-70 shows a way to play the scale up and down while still following the "rule." In addition you should create full-range versions in this key of examples 1-31, 1-33, 1-35, 1-37 and 1-39.

Ex.1-71 is a practice loop for this fingerboard pattern that works on all the same chords mentioned in ex.1-47.

The Cmi-maj7 hexatonic scale fingering and exercises in the twelfth position

Ex.1-72 shows a practical fingerboard pattern for playing the Cmi-maj7 hexatonic scale in the twelfth position.

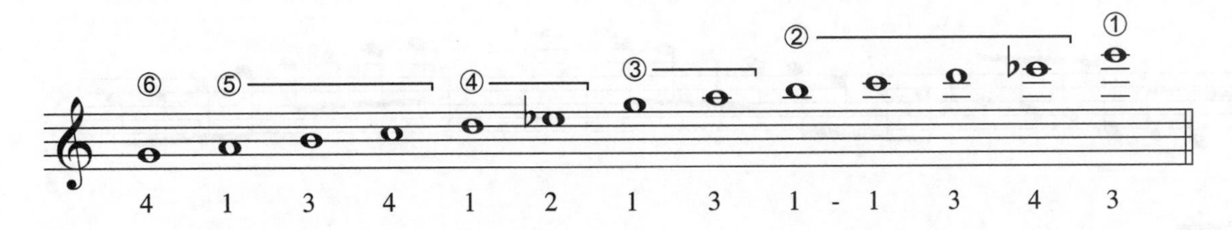

Ex.1-73 shows a way to play the scale up and down while still following the "rule." In addition you should create full-range versions in this key of examples 1-32, 1-34, 1-36, 1-38 and 1-40.

Ex.1-74 is a practice loop for this fingerboard pattern that works on all the same chords mentioned in ex.1-50.

Long Three-Octave Fingerboard Patterns

The fingerboard patterns that follow will use some relatively easy position shifts and finger stretches to extend the range of our hexatonic scales through three octaves. You'll notice that the fingerboard shapes and fingerings are replicated exactly in each of the three octaves, making them surprisingly easy to learn. There may be many other practical patterns possible that use this method, and you should feel free to develop as many of them on your own as you like, but I'm only going to show a few of my favorites to get you started. The three octaves lie on three sets of two consecutive strings: the bottom two, the middle two, and the top two.

Cmaj7-Ami7 hexatonic from G in a "two-plus-four" pattern

Ex.1-75 shows the pattern and fingering for the Cmaj7-Ami7 hexatonic scale with G as the lowest note and using what I'll call a "two-plus-four" pattern, meaning that first we have two notes on the sixth string followed by four notes on the fifth string, adding up to all six. As we play the last two notes of the six, notice that the hand is already in position to play the same six notes an octave higher on the middle two strings using the same "two-plus-four" pattern and fingering, etc.

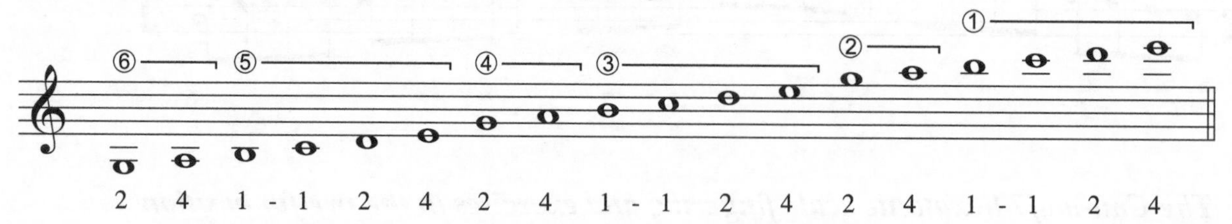

Ex.1-76 shows a way to play the scale ascending and descending.

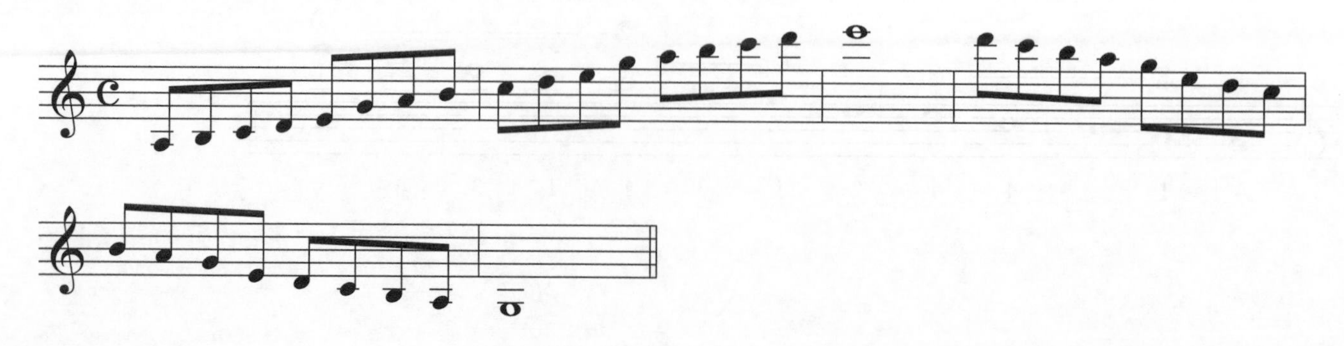

Ex.1-77 shows a practice loop that can be played in this fingerboard pattern.

Cmi-maj7 hexatonic from G in a "two-plus-four" pattern

Ex.1-78 shows the Cmi-maj7 hexatonic scale with G as the lowest note, again using a "two-plus-four" configuration.

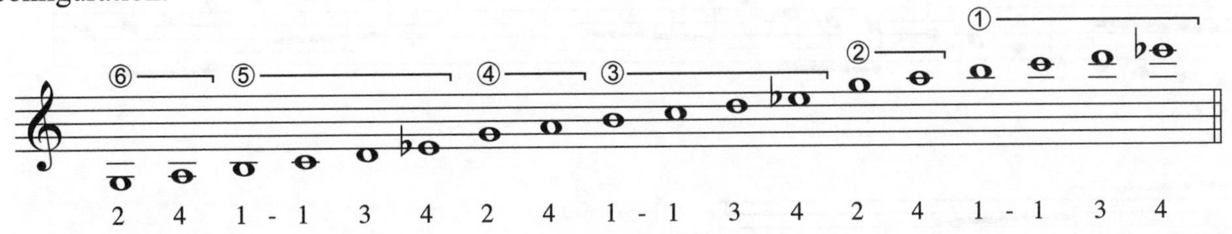

Ex.1-79 shows a way to play the scale ascending and descending.

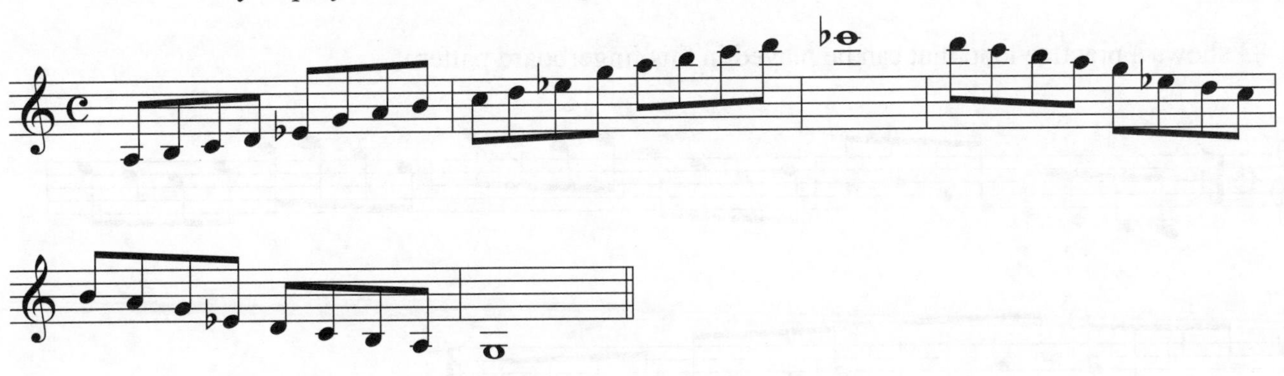

Ex.1-80 shows a practice loop that can be played in this fingerboard pattern.

Cmaj7-Ami7 hexatonic from G in a "four-plus-two" pattern

Ex.1-81 shows the pattern and fingering for the Cmaj7-Ami7 hexatonic scale with G as the lowest note, this time using a "four-plus-two" pattern with four notes on the sixth string followed by two notes on the fifth string, then repeating on the middle two strings and the top two strings.

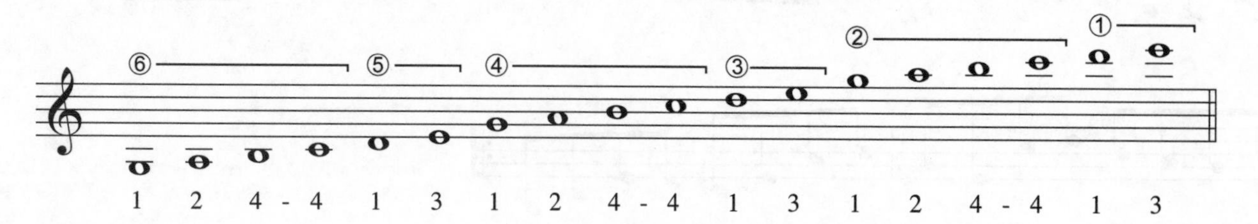

Ex.1-82 shows a way to play the scale ascending and descending.

Ex.1-83 shows a practice loop that can be played in this fingerboard pattern.

Cmi-maj7 hexatonic from G in a "four-plus-two" pattern

Ex.1-84 shows the Cmi-maj7 hexatonic scale with G as the lowest note and using a "four-plus-two" pattern.

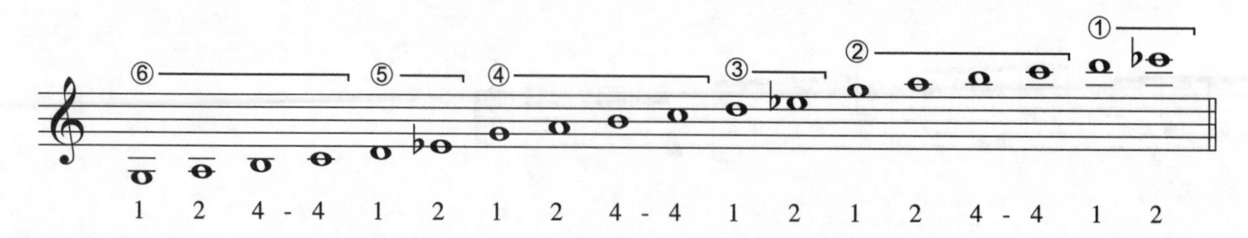

Ex.1-85 shows a way to play the scale ascending and descending.

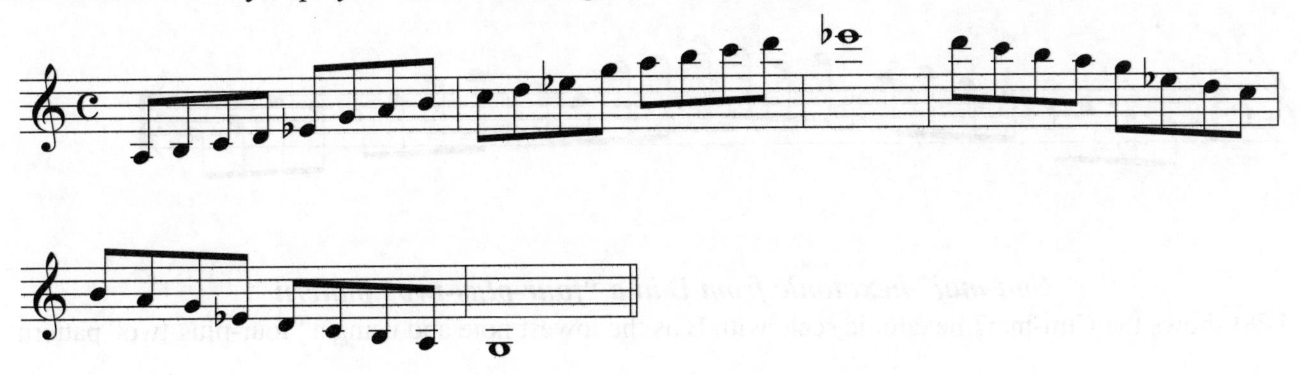

Ex.1-86 shows a practice loop that can be played in this fingerboard pattern.

Cmaj7-Ami7 hexatonic from B in a "four-plus-two" pattern

Ex.1-87 shows the pattern and fingering for the Cmaj7-Ami7 hexatonic scale with B as the lowest note and using a "four-plus-two" pattern.

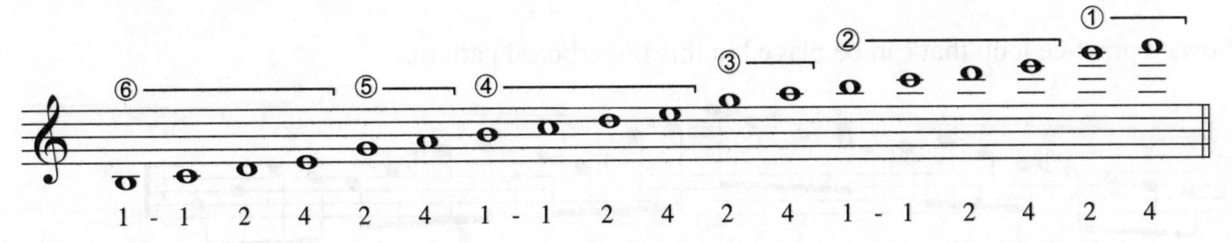

Ex.1-88 shows a way to play the scale ascending and descending.

Ex.1-89 shows a practice loop that can be played in this fingerboard pattern.

Cmi-maj7 hexatonic from B in a "four-plus-two" pattern

Ex.1-90 shows the Cmi-maj7 hexatonic scale with B as the lowest note and using a "four-plus-two" pattern.

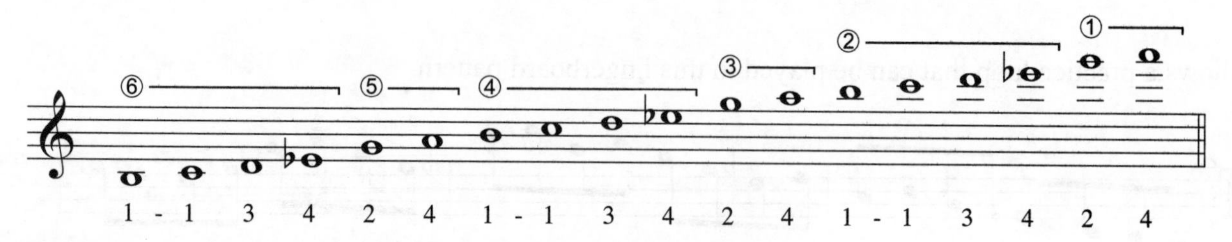

Ex.1-91 shows a way to play the scale ascending and descending.

Ex.1-92 shows a practice loop that can be played in this fingerboard pattern.

Cmaj7-Ami7 hexatonic from D in a "two-plus-four" pattern

Ex.1-93 shows the pattern and fingering for the Cmaj7-Ami7 hexatonic scale with D as the lowest note and using a "two-plus-four" pattern.

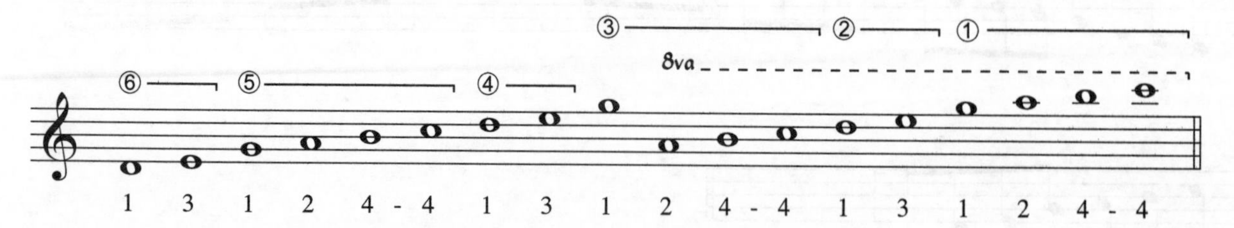

Ex.1-94 shows a way to play the scale ascending and descending.

Ex.1-95 shows a practice loop that can be played in this fingerboard pattern.

Cmi-maj7 hexatonic from D in a "two-plus-four" pattern

Ex.1-96 shows the pattern and fingering for the Cmi-maj7 hexatonic scale with D as the lowest note and using a "two-plus-four" pattern.

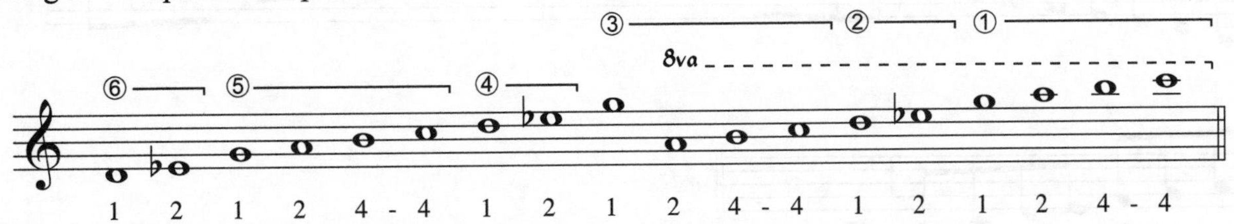

Ex.1-97 shows a way to play the scale ascending and descending.

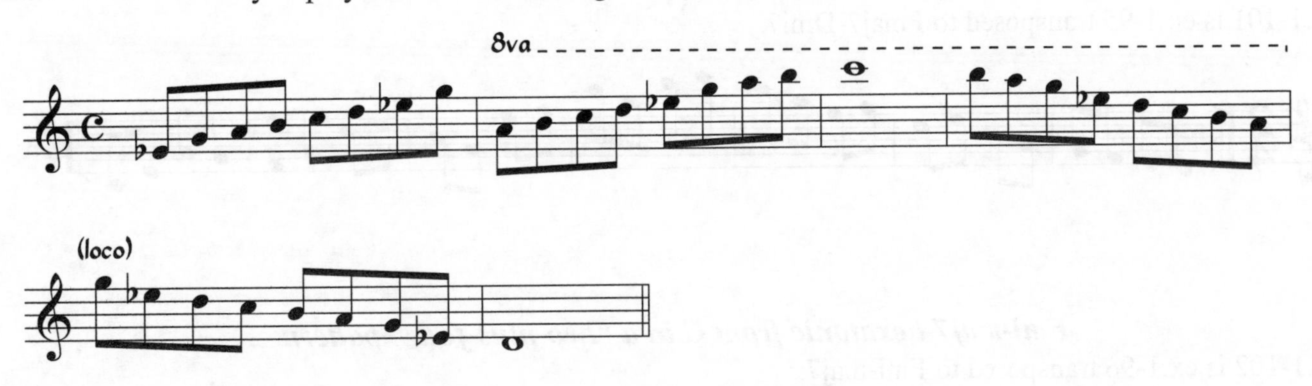

Ex.1-98 shows a practice loop that can be played in this fingerboard pattern.

Range limitations and transposition

Ex.1-93 through 1-98 are playable on guitars with 20 or more frets and a cutaway, but on other guitars it may be necessary to change to another key (transpose) in order to learn the patterns and fingerings for those examples. Actually, we're going to have to learn to change keys anyway because I'm not going to write out all of the previous examples in all keys, so we may as well learn how to do it now (if you don't know already). All the forms we've looked at so far use no open strings and are therefore movable, making transposition easy. Let's look at ex.1-93 through 1-98 transposed to Fmaj7-Dmi7 hexatonic and Fmi-maj7 hexatonic.

Fmaj7-Dmi7 hexatonic from G in a "two-plus-four" pattern

Ex.1-99 is ex.1-93 transposed to Fmaj7-Dmi7.

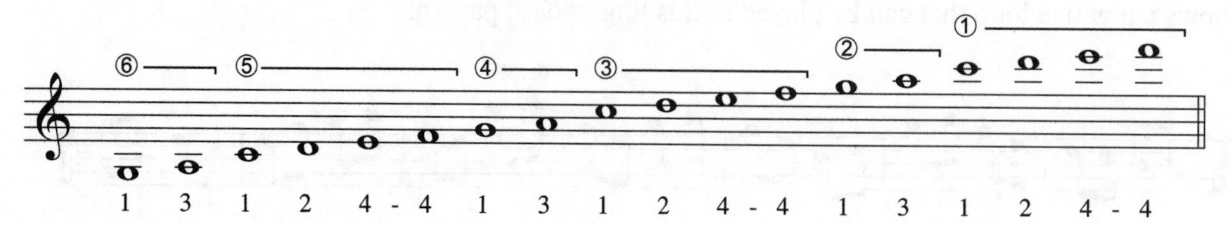

Ex.1-100 is ex.1-94 transposed to Fmaj7-Dmi7.

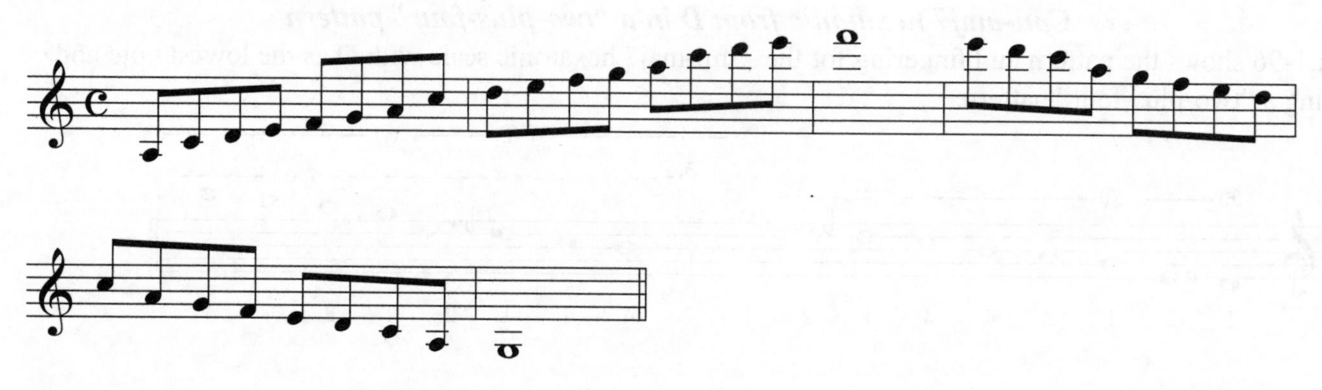

Ex.1-101 is ex.1-95 transposed to Fmaj7-Dmi7.

Fmi-maj7 hexatonic from G in a "two-plus-four" pattern

Ex.1-102 is ex.1-96 transposed to Fmi-maj7.

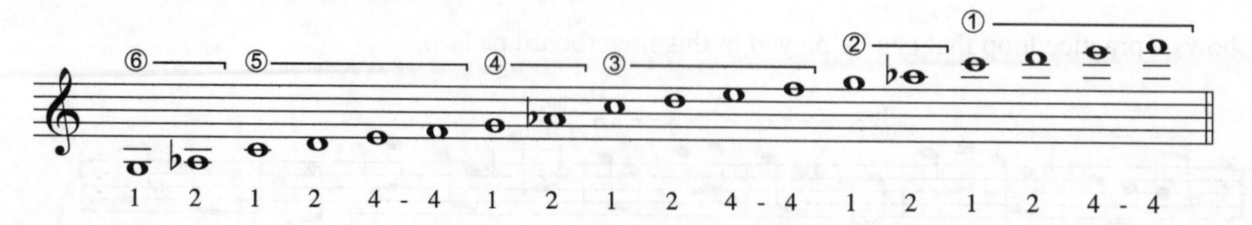

Ex.1-103 is ex.1-97 transposed to Fmi-maj7.

Ex.1-104 is ex.1-98 transposed to Fmi-maj7.

By the way, "three-plus-three" also adds up to six, so if you want to try creating alternate patterns and fingerings, that might be a place to start.

Some Thoughts on HOW to Practice the Exercises

I've just given you a lot of stuff to practice, so now might be a good time to share some thoughts on HOW to practice in order to get the maximum benefit from the exercises.

First of all, it's a good idea to break things down and practice small amounts with focus on the fine details, and don't worry that it seems there's too much you're not getting to. Patience is key. If you chip away on bite-size pieces they will eventually accumulate into a vast amount of useful material.

If you're working on a new pattern you can learn it in fragments first. Try to focus on the two-note cells. Once the fingers start "getting" the pattern, you could play it once in whatever key places it the lowest (toward the nut) on the fingerboard, then play it again one fret higher, thinking the names of the chords it fits, then another fret higher, and so on up the fingerboard as far as you can go. For example, let's say you're working on ex.1-53. As you begin to memorize the pattern, take it down to the second and first positions. As you play it there, think "Amaj13, F#mi11, Dmaj13#11, and B13sus". Then move it up a fret, play and think "Bbmaj13, Gmi11, Ebmaj13#11, and C13sus", etc. up the fingerboard.

Take your time and make sure you hear *all* the notes intended and *only* the notes intended, and evenly in time. Don't worry about the other patterns you're not getting to yet. There will be plenty of other days for those.

Once you get a lot of patterns and exercises down, it might be cool to shift tactics and play all the studies once each in one key everyday, doing a new key each day, perhaps going around the cycle of fifths. This way you'll do them all in every key in twelve days. By then you should have them for life, at least with a little "brush-up" now and then, so you could move on to something new and less familiar.

Applying the Hexatonics to Altered V7 Chords Resolving to I Chords

Now that we have material to practice and an idea about how to practice it, we should take a look at how to start applying the hexatonic lines to jazz improvisation. Many students through the years have asked for help in making a breakthrough in the ability to improvise over altered dominant chords, so I'll share a method I used to address that same problem for myself. First, it occurred to me that altered dominant chords most often resolve to some kind of I chord that the altered chord is the V of (such as G7alt going to some kind of C chord, be it major or minor or another dominant-type chord), so we should practice resolving the lines to the following chord. I'll start with 8th note lines filling a measure in 4/4 time and landing on a target chord tone in the resolution chord. Let's stick to a few basic lines that generally follow the rules we used above.

Descending lines resolving to the third of the I chord

Ex.1-105 starts on the root of a G7alt and descends the Abmi-maj7 hexatonic scale, bringing us smoothly to an easy landing on E, the major 3rd of Cmaj7 or C7. If the chord of resolution is Cmi7 or Cmi-maj7 or Cmi6 (or Cmi *anything*), just change the E to Eb.

Ex.1-106 resolves the same way, but starts on the b7th of the G7alt by reversing the order of the first two notes from the previous example.

Descending lines resolving to the fifth of the I chord

Ex.1-107 starts on the #9 of the G7alt and descends the Abmi-maj7 hexatonic scale, bringing us smoothly to an easy landing on G, the 5th of Cmaj7, C7, or the various Cmi chords. In the less common event that the chord of resolution is Cmi7b5 or C7alt, just change the G to Gb.

Ex.1-108 also resolves to the 5th of C, but starts on the b9 of the G7alt by reversing the order of the first two notes from the previous example.

Descending lines resolving to the ninth of the I chord

Ex.1-109 starts on the b13th of G7alt and descends the Abmi-maj7 hexatonic scale, resolving to D, the 9th of C maj7, dom7, mi-maj7, mi7, and mi7b5. If the chord of resolution is C7alt, change the D to C natural.

Ex.1-110 also resolves to the 9th of C, but starts on the note Cb, functioning as the major 3rd of the G7alt, by reversing the order of the first two notes from the previous example.

Ascending lines resolving to the third of the I chord

Ex.1-111 starts on the b7th of G7alt and ascends to a resolution on the 3rd of the C chord. Again, if it's Cmi, change the last note to Eb.

Ex.1-112 starts on the root of G7alt by reversing the order of the first two notes from the previous example.

Ascending lines resolving to the fifth of the I chord

Ex.1-113 starts on the b9 of G7alt and ascends to a resolution on the 5th of the C chord.

Ex.1-114 starts on the #9 of G7alt by reversing the order of the first two notes from the previous example.

Ascending lines resolving to the ninth of the I chord

Ex.1-115 starts on the note Cb, functioning as the major 3rd of the G7alt, and ascends to a resolution on the 9th of the C chord.

Ex.1-116 starts on the b13 of G7alt by reversing the order of the first two notes from the previous example.

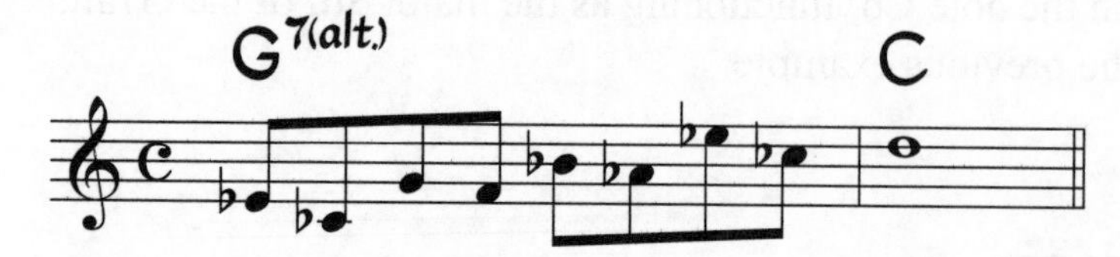

Other variations

Ex.1-117 starts on the root of G7alt and begins a descent which is interrupted by skipping up to the next higher two-note cell before resuming a smooth descent to an easy landing on the 5th of the C chord.

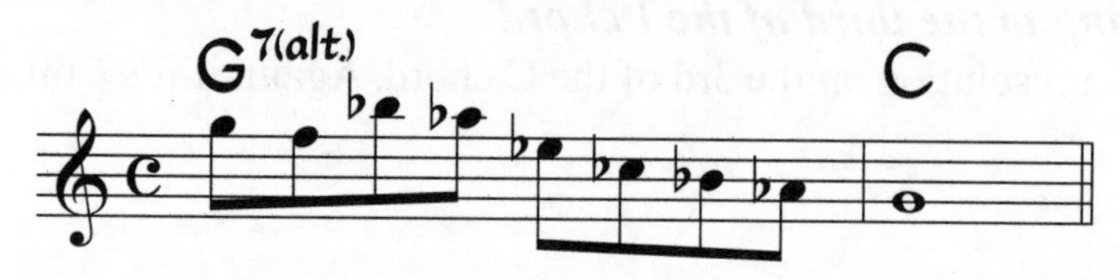

Ex.1-118 starts on the b7th of G7alt by reversing the order of the first two notes from the previous example.

Ex.1-119 starts on the #9 of G7alt and begins a descent which is interrupted by skipping up to the next higher two-note cell before resuming a smooth descent to a nice resolution to the 9th of the C chord.

Ex.1-120 starts on the b9 of G7alt by reversing the order of the first two notes from the previous example.

Ex.1-121 starts on the b13 of G7alt and begins a descent which is interrupted by skipping up to the next higher two-note cell before resuming a smooth descent to an easy landing on the 3rd of the C chord.

Ex.1-122 starts on the note Cb, functioning as the major 3rd of the G7alt, by reversing the order of the first two notes from the previous example.

These examples gave me tremendous confidence in improvising on altered dominant chords resolving to their intended tonics because they provided an arsenal of pleasantly melodic lines that flowed effortlessly into the following chord.

By the way, keep in mind that all of these lines fit perfectly over the tritone substitute chord for G7, the Db13#11(natural 9). The analysis of the starting notes of course will change. For example, if a line started on the root of G7alt, that same line starts on the #11 of Db7.

Applying Hexatonics to Complete II-V-I Progressions

Next let's explore lines on the essential II-V-I progression using maj7-mi7 hexatonic scales on the II and the I, and mi-maj7 hexatonic scales on the altered V. The examples will be shown in the key of C, so the II chord will feature the Fmaj7-Dmi7 hexatonic scale, the V chord will feature the Abmi-maj7 hexatonic scale, and the I chord, of course, the Cmaj7-Ami7 hexatonic scale.

I'll start by showing several variations that all start with an identical first measure beginning on the root of the Dmi7, but each continuing in a unique way.

Ascending from the root of the II chord

Ex.1-123 starts on the root of Dmi7 and ascends a simple hexatonic idea followed by a simple descending hexatonic over the G7alt that starts on the b13 and resolves to the 9 of Cmaj7 with an ascending line.

Ex.1-124 has the same first measure and third measure, but re-orders the notes on the altered chord.

Ex.1-125 has the same first measure but uses new variations on the last two bars.

Ex.1-126 has the same first measure and third measure as the last example, but re-orders the notes on the altered chord.

Ex.1-127 uses a different re-ordering of the notes in the second bar.

Ex.1-128 has the same first measure as the last example, but continues a new way. Notice that it's identical to the Joe Pass line shown in ex.1-18 except that here we continue on the I chord.

Ascending from the ninth of the II chord

If you would like to try some lines starting on the 9th of the Dmi7, simply reverse the order of the first two notes on any of the II-V-I examples above that started on the root.

I'm not going to show as many variations on the following examples because after just a few I'm sure you'll get the idea and will be able to improvise your own variations.

Ascending from the third of the II chord

Next let's check out some lines that ascend from the b3rd of the Dmi7 chord.

Ex.1-129 starts by ascending from F, the b3rd of the II chord, and finishes with the same second and third measures as ex.1-123.

Ex.1-130 has the same first measure as the last example and continues with a new combination.

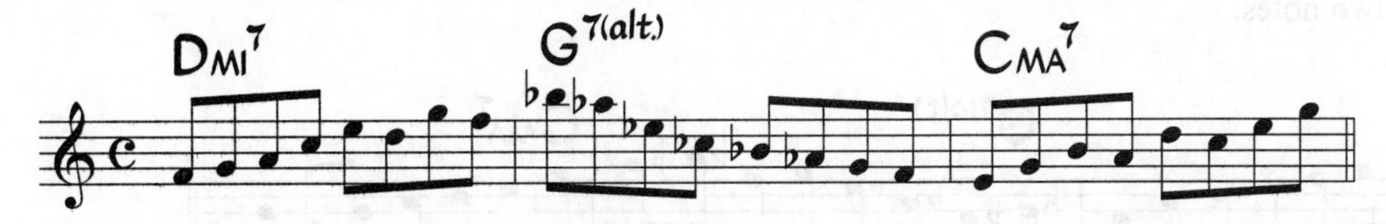

Ex.1-131 has the same first measure as the last example followed by yet another variation.

Ascending from the eleventh of the II chord

If you would like to try some lines starting on the 11th of the Dmi7, simply reverse the order of the first two notes on any of the II-V-I examples above that started on the b3rd.

Now we'll try a line that ascends from the 5th of Dmi7.

Ascending from the fifth of the II chord

Ex.1-132 ascends from A, the 5th of Dm7. Look for your own variations.

Ascending from the seventh of the II chord

If you'd like to ascend from the b7th of Dmi7 (the note C), reverse the order of the first two notes of a line that ascended from the 5th.

By now you might be wondering about lines that start by descending on the II chord. Let's check some out.

Descending from the ninth and root of the II chord

Ex.1-133 descends from the 9th of Dmi7. Find variations. To start on the root of the II chord, reverse the order of the first two notes.

Descending from the seventh and fifth of the II chord

Ex.1-134 descends from the b7th of Dmi7. Find variations. To start on the fifth of the II chord, reverse the order of the first two notes.

Descending from the eleventh and third of the II chord

Ex.1-135 starts by descending from the 11th of Dmi7. Look for variations. To start on the b3rd of the II chord, you can simply reverse the order of the first two notes, or you could look deeper into re-ordering the notes for more interesting results (homework assignment for you).

Applying Hexatonics Using the 13susb9 Sound and its Harmonic Implications

Go back and take a look at ex.1-26 through 1-29, demonstrating the use of the Fmi-maj7 hexatonic scale over the G7 chord, which implies the sound of G13susb9. Since the sub-dominant of C is F, this is actually functioning as a sub-dominant minor. This means that the II-V-I lines using the V13susb9 sound can actually fit a variety of commonly used progressions. All the chords shown in the left column below are theoretically interchangeable, as are all the chords in the right column, and any of those chord combinations going on to C major work with the lines from 1-27 through 1-29 as well as the two examples to follow.

Dmi7	G13susb9
Fmaj7	Fmi-maj7
F6	Fmi6
G13sus	Bb13#11

Ex.1-136 starts on the b3rd of Dmi7 (the root of Fmaj7) and demonstrates the use of the sub-dominant minor hexatonic scale.

Ex.1-137 descends from the 9th of Dmi7 (the 7th of Fmaj7), also demonstrating the sub-dominant minor sound.

By now you should know how to go about re-combining the line fragments we've been using into many more variations using the sub-dominant minor sound.

Applying Hexatonics to II-V-I in Minor Tonality

Let's check out a very interesting way to apply hexatonic scales to II-V-I in minor. We'll use the key of C minor to demonstrate. The changes will be Dmi7b5 to G7alt to Cmi-maj7. The scales will be Fmi-maj7 hexatonic on the Dmi7b5, Abmi-maj7 hexatonic on the G7alt, and Cmi-maj7 hexatonic on the Cmi-maj7. Notice that they're all mi-maj7 hexatonics. Going from the II to the V the scale moves up a minor 3rd, while going from the V to the I the scale moves up a major 3rd.

Ex.1-138 ascends from the root of Dmi7b5. To start from 9th of the II chord, reverse the order of the first two notes.

Ex.1-139 ascends from the b3rd of Dmi7b5. To start from 11th of the II chord, reverse the order of the first two notes.

Ex.1-140 ascends from the b5th of Dmi7b5. To start from 7th of the II chord, reverse the order of the first two notes (and possibly the second two note cell as well).

Ex.1-141 descends from the 9th of Dmi7b5. To start from root of the II chord, reverse the order of the first two notes.

Ex.1-142 descends from the b7th of Dmi7b5. To start from b5th of the II chord, reverse the order of the first two notes.

Ex.1-143 descends from the 11th of Dmi7b5. To start from b3rd of the II chord, reverse the order of the first two notes.

Incidentally, minor tonality II-Vs sometimes resolve to major chords (Dmi7b5-G7alt-Cmaj7 for instance). Some examples of well-known standards that do this would include Cole Porter's "What Is This Thing Called Love" and "I Love You," and Victor Young's "Stella By Starlight." I really don't need to write out any examples because all you have to do is change all the Eb notes from the third bar of each minor tonality II-V-I to E naturals and you'll have it.

Applying Hexatonics with Cycle Motion

The minor tonality II-V-Is moved mi-maj7 hexatonics up by minor and major thirds. There are also cadences where the mi-maj7 hexatonics move around the cycle (down in fifths or up in fourths). For example, the II chord in the II-V-I in a minor blues is frequently changed into a bVIdom7 (in C minor: Ab13#11 to G7alt to Cmi). The bass notes could change, changing the chord names without changing the scales or lines played over them. An example would be D7alt to Db13#11 to Cmi.

I'm only going to show two examples, so it's up to you to discover more.

Ex.1-144 starts by ascending from the 3rd of the Ab13#11. To start on the #11, reverse the order of the first two notes.

Ex.1-145 starts on the 7th of Ab13#11. To start on the 9th, reverse the order of the first two notes.

Try making the last chord major instead of minor as another useful variation.

Applying Hexatonics with Descending Half-Step Motion

Now we've done motion by thirds and by cycle. Some progressions suggest descending half-step motion. In C major, one example would be D13#11 to Db13#11 to Cmaj7 (applicable to Duke Ellington's "Satin Doll" among many others). A change of bass note could make it D13#11 to G7alt to Cmaj7, but the half-step motion of the hexatonics remains unchanged.

Again, I'm only showing two examples. The rest is up to you.

Ex.1-146 starts by ascending from the 3rd of the D13#11. To start on the #11, reverse the order of the first two notes.

Ex.1-147 starts by descending from the 13th of the D13#11. To start on the 5th, reverse the order of the first two notes.

Applying Hexatonics with Tritone Motion

If we stay on a dominant chord for two bars before resolving to the tonic chord, the quality of the dominant can change from 13#11 to altered, implying movement by a tritone. In C major, G13#11 becomes G7alt, implying Dmi-maj7 hexatonic going to Abmi-maj7 hexatonic.

Only two examples again. You know what to do.

Ex.1-148 starts by ascending from the 5th of the G13#11. To start on the 13th, reverse the order of the first two notes.

Ex.1-149 starts by descending from the 13th of the G13#11. To start on the 5th, reverse the order of the first two notes.

"Editing" Eighth-Note Lines

All the lines we've been playing pretty much fill each measure with a steady string of eighth-notes. The eighth-note is the basic rhythmic unit of improvised jazz lines. Ultimately, however, we want our improvisations to "breathe." Lines need some spaces to highlight and frame the actual content.

Look back at ex.1-3 from Joe Pass. The spaces help shape the meaning of the notes. Looking at the third and fourth measures, I imagine that this phrase is an "edited" version of ex.1-150.

Ex.1-151 is ex.1-150 with all the notes that Joe didn't play replaced by rests.

Ex.1-152 adds a couple of tricks. First, the Cb in bar one has been moved into the rest that was on the "and" of beat two. This is a form of anticipation that helps propel the line forward. Second, the Bb at the beginning or bar two can now be a quarter-note. The result is the line as Joe played it.

You can see that a few edits and adjustments can make a difference so I suggest you try some similar strategies with at least some of the lines we've been doing.

Applying Hexatonics to II-V-I in Three-Four Time

Three-four time is very important so we should try adapting our hexatonic lines to this time signature. I'll show two examples that start with the same first measure to demonstrate that variations are still practical. Many more are possible, so you know what to do.

Ex.1-153 and ex.1-154 both start by ascending from the root of Dmi7. To start on the 9th, reverse the order of the first two notes.

Ex.1-155 and ex.1-156 both start by ascending from the b3rd of Dmi7. To start on the 11th, reverse the order of the first two notes.

Ex.1-157 and ex.1-158 both start by ascending from the 5th of Dmi7. To start on the 7th, reverse the order of the first two notes.

There will only be one example for each line that begins by descending, but try variations.

Ex.1-159 starts by descending from the 9th of Dmi7. To start on the root, reverse the order of the first two notes.

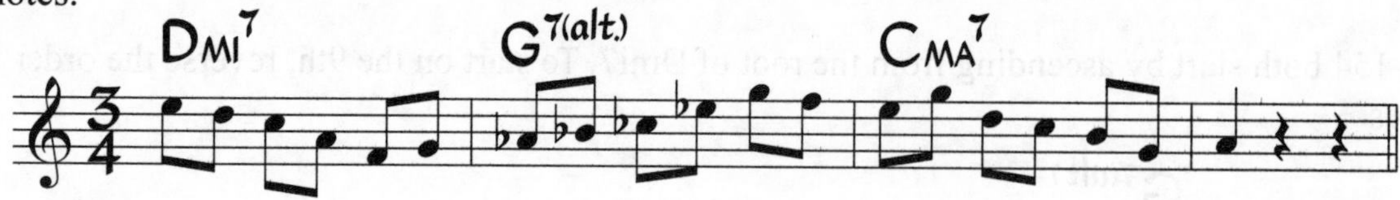

Ex.1-160 starts by descending from the 11th of Dmi7. To start on the 3rd, reverse the order of the first two notes.

Ex.1-161 starts by descending from the b7th of Dmi7. To start on the 5th, reverse the order of the first two notes.

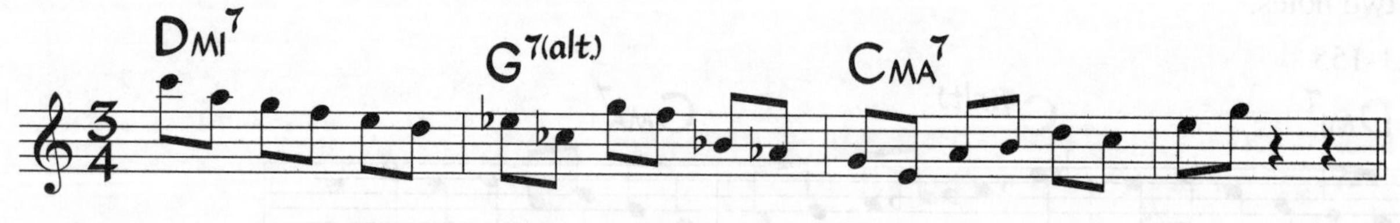

You should be able to convert these into minor tonalities and create three-four versions of the other progressions we've done, so do it.

Applying Hexatonics to II-V-I with Only Two Beats Per Change

When there are only two beats of any given chord, there is only enough time for four eighth-notes, so it would seem that hexatonic improvisation should be impossible. Actually we can still create many great lines that are limited to notes from the hexatonics even though we don't use all of them. I'll show two examples that start with the same first two beats to demonstrate that variations are still practical.

Ex.1-162 and ex.1-163 both start by ascending from the root of Dmi7. To start on the 9th, reverse the order of the first two notes.

Ex.1-164 and ex.1-165 both start by ascending from the b3rd of Dmi7. To start on the 11th, reverse the order of the first two notes.

Ex.1-166 and ex.1-167 both start by ascending from the 5th of Dmi7. To start on the 7th, reverse the order of the first two notes.

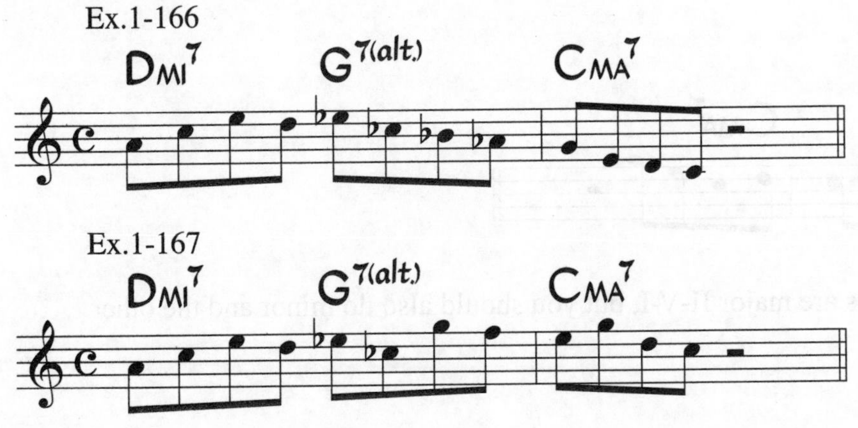

Ex.1-168 and ex.1-169 both start by descending from the 9th of Dmi7. To start on the root, reverse the order of the first two notes.

Ex.1-170 and ex.1-171 both start by descending from the11th of Dmi7. To start on the 3rd, reverse the order of the first two notes.

Ex.1-172 and ex.1-173 both start by descending from the b7th of Dmi7. To start on the 5th, reverse the order of the first two notes.

All these two-beat-per-change examples are major II-V-I, but you should also do minor and the other progressions with two beat changes.

Fingering and Rhythmic Variations

Some fingering variations

Take a look back at ex.1-18 from Joe Pass. We'll use this line to explore some possible fingering variations. All of the examples will start with the same finger at the same place on the fingerboard and then move in different ways to demonstrate some possibilities. You should try the same process starting with other fingers and in various positions, and also try the same process on all the other lines you're practicing.

Ex.1-174 shows the line played entirely in the second and third positions. It starts with the fourth finger on the fifth string and moves straight across the fingerboard and back.

Ex.1-175 starts out the same but uses the first two descending whole-steps that sequence up by minor thirds to shift along the second string to the sixth position.

Ex.1-176 starts out the same and also climbs to the sixth position, but shifts along the fourth string using a slide and a slight finger stretch.

Ex.1-177 starts out the same as ex.1-175 but uses all three descending whole-steps that sequence up by minor thirds to shift along the second string to the eighth position.

Ex.1-178 starts out the same as ex.1-176 and the uses the last two descending whole-steps that sequence up by minor thirds to shift along the second string to the eighth position. It finishes using some slides to descend back to the fifth position.

Hopefully these examples will inspire you to try using the lines to move around the fingerboard and get "out of the box." I've found that reducing the number of strings a line is played on generally makes it easier to play and to play with good jazz articulation. It also greatly increases the range that will be available to you.

Some rhythmic variations

Let's continue using the same line to experiment with some rhythmic variations. In general a jazz line will sound less "square" if it doesn't start or end on a down-beat.

Ex.1-179 starts on the "and" of one (the anticipation of two) and catches up by using a triplet. I've added an eighth-note at the end so the phrase ends off the beat. These minor changes gives the line a more interesting shape.

Ex.1-180 starts on the "and" of four in the previous measure, which is the anticipation of one. This is followed by an eighth-rest right on beat one so the rest of the line can continue as it was. Hearing the first two eighth-notes off the beat gives the forward motion some extra propulsion.

Ex.1-181 starts with the first three eighth-notes off the beat, starting on the "and" of four in the previous measure. This is achieved by omitting the first note and starting on the E so the timing will work out right.

Ex.1-182 starts out like 181 but, in the second bar, omits a note and anticipates the next, similar to what was discussed in the section on "editing".

Another way to add rhythmic excitement to a line is to use some strings of triplets (if the tempo isn't too fast). Two beats of triplets is six notes, and so is three beats of eighth-notes, so we could try using some of our three-four lines converted into triplets. This is demonstrated in the next example.

Ex.1-183 starts out like 1-18 for two beats. Now look at ex.1-158 in three-four. The first two bars of that example are converted into triplets and used in our current example on the last two beats of bar one and the first two beats of bar two. The next two beats are like 1-18 again. The phrase ends with a new idea using a triplet and ending off the beat.

The Compatibility of Hexatonics with Wholetone and Diminished Scales

The well-known wholetone scale is, as I'm sure you know, a scale of six notes and therefore a hexatonic scale. Played over dominant-type chords the wholetone has no avoid notes, a feature shared by the other hexatonics we've been playing.

Ex.1-184 shows a hexatonic II-V-I line using the G wholetone scale over the G7alt5.

The eight-note diminished scale is not hexatonic, but used correctly over dominant-type chords it also has no avoid notes like the other hexatonics we've been playing. The eight notes can also be divided into four sets of two-note cells (the whole-steps) to generate melodies that are quite similar in character to the hexatonic lines we've been doing. Ex.1-185 shows a hexatonic II-V-I line using the eight-note diminished scale over the G13b9.

Ex.1-186 shows another variation.

A Sample Chorus on a Popular Standard Demonstrating Hexatonics

Ex.1-187 shows a hypothetical improvisation over one chorus of a popular standard tune that all jazz musicians know. It's almost 100% material covered in this chapter, so you can do your own analysis.

I think that about covers the conventional hexatonics, so let's move on.

Chapter 2 – Using Chromatics to Improvise "Inside" Conventional Chords

This chapter introduces the use of chromatics for conventional improvisation that actually sounds "inside" the chords, as opposed to using chromatics for "outside" playing on chord changes or "free" playing without chord changes, both of which we'll get to in our next book. This introduction will mainly deal with one chord at a time with a few exceptions, such as an occasional II-V-I, or ex.2-48, which treats rhythm changes as if it were really just one chord. Dealing with longer ideas across multiple chord changes will come later so by then we can use "every trick in the book."

Let's start by looking at some lines that add a few chromatic notes to the hexatonic lines we worked on in the last chapter.

Chromatics Added to Hexatonic Lines

Some actual examples of chromatics added to hexatonics

Play ex.2-1, an excerpt from a Pat Martino solo. It descends an Ami7 hexatonic scale and ends by adding a Bb and an Ab to "fill-in" the major 3rd from the 9th down to the b7th. This is a specific device that Pat seems fond of using.

Ex.2-2, also from Pat Martino, is another demonstration of the same specific device.

Now play ex.2-3, Pat Martino using the chromatically-enhanced hexatonic scale on a maj7 chord. It descends an Fmaj7 hexatonic scale and adds an Eb and a Db to "fill-in" the major 3rd from the 7th down to the 5th. As you know, each maj7 hexatonic scale is the same as its relative mi7 hexatonic scale. In this case the relative minor of F is D minor, so the added chromatics in D minor would fill-in the major 3rd from the 9th of Dmi7 down to the b7th, the same as in the previous two examples.

Ex.2-4 shows another Pat Martino line on Fmaj7 using the same specific device, but using an "edit" in the first and second beats of the second measure.

Ex.2-5 shows what I believe would be the "unedited" version of the descending portion of ex.2-4.

Keep in mind that the Fmaj7 lines can be used on Fmaj7, Dmi7, Bbmaj7#11, and G13sus.

Ex.2-6 shows 2-5 converted to Fmi-maj7 by simply flatting all the A notes. This line works for Abmaj7#5, Fmi-maj7, Dmi9b5, Bb13#11, G13susb9, and E7alt.

Ex.2-7 comes from Bruce Foreman descending on a G7alt chord resolving into C major, using the chromatically-enhanced Abmi-maj7 hexatonic scale.

Notice that the chromatics were always used descending. In theory any major 3rd could be filled in chromatically ascending or descending. In this hexatonic context, however, the descending version sounds best.

Fingerings and exercises for adding chromatics to positional hexatonics

Now we need some fingerings and studies to help us get ready for our own application of these chromatically-enhanced hexatonics. Let's start by working with some of the positional fingerings we did in Chapter 1.

Ex.2-8 is based on ex.1-47 in Cmaj7-Ami7. The first three bars are the same. Then the line descends using the added chromatics. The suggested strings and fingerings are shown. Ex.1-47 was a practice loop while this line is not in the given form.

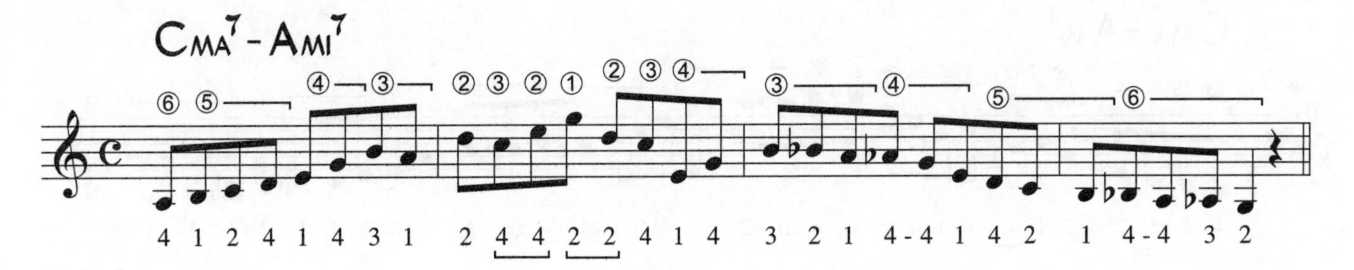

Ex.2-9 is based on ex.1-50, the same as 2-8 but converted into Cmi-maj7 by lowering all the E's to Eb.

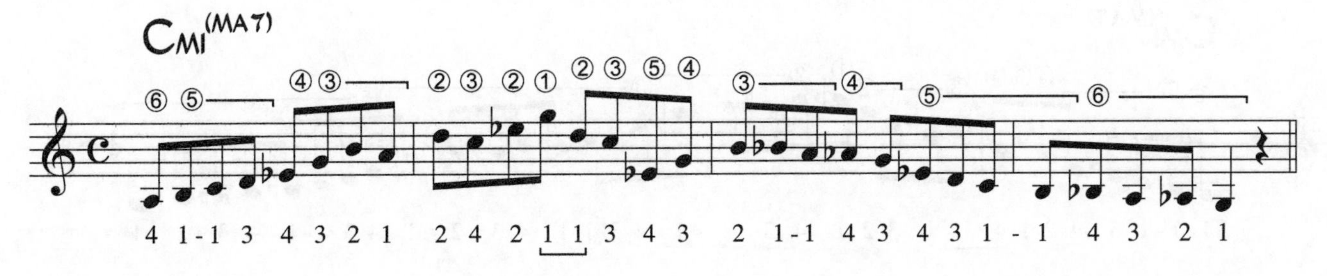

Ex.2-10 is based on ex.1-53 in Cmaj7-Ami7.

Ex.2-11 is based on ex.1-56 in Cmi-maj7.

Your assignment now is to use these examples to add the descending chromatics to ex.1-59, 1-62, 1-65, 1-68, 1-71, and 1-74, covering all the positional forms shown in Chapter 1.

Adding chromatics to the long three-octave fingerboard patterns

Ex.2-12 is based on ex.1-77, a long "two-plus-four" fingerboard pattern in Cmaj7-Ami7 using the descending chromatics.

Ex.2-13 is based on ex.1-80, a long "two-plus-four" fingerboard pattern in Cmi-maj7 using the descending chromatics.

Ex.2-14 is based on ex.1-83, a long "four-plus-two" fingerboard pattern in Cmaj7-Ami7 using the descending chromatics.

Ex.2-15 is based on ex.1-86, a long "four-plus-two" fingerboard pattern in Cmi-maj7 using the descending chromatics.

Now your assignment is to add the descending chromatics to the remaining long three-octave fingerboard patterns from Chapter 1.

Using Other Chromatic Notes Added to Hexatonic Lines

Of course there are many other chromatic notes that can be added to hexatonic lines in various ways.

Some actual recorded examples

Look at ex.2-16, a typical Joe Pass line that is all hexatonic except for a quick ascending and descending chromatic passage in triplets filling in the minor 3rd between the 7th and the 9th of Cmaj7.

Ex.2-17, also from Joe, shows him filling in the major 3rd between the 5th and the b3rd of Dmi7 with descending chromatics.

Pat Martino also descends chromatically from the 5th to the b3rd of a mi7 chord in ex.2-18. This is a II-V-I phrase that is not really hexatonic, but in addition to demonstrating the 5th to b3rd chromatic descent on mi7, it also demonstrates a new and very important device in measure three on the I chord, Gmaj7. The line descends from the 5th, D, to the non-hexatonic 4th, C, before going up chromatically from A through A# and finally resolving on the 3rd, B.

Ex.2-19 shows Pat Martino using the same device in an otherwise pure hexatonic line on Gmaj7. This time the device starts the phrase before continuing hexatonically.

In ex.2-20 Jimmy Raney uses this device in an otherwise hexatonic (actually pentatonic) line.

Since the device starts on the 5th and resolves two beats later on the 3rd, we could call it a "5-to-3 device."

Because it resolves after two beats, it could actually come two beats *before* the chord change actually arrives, a form of anticipation.

George Benson shows us how in ex.2-21, a II-V-I in Eb major (Fmi7-Bb7alt-Ebmaj7). He starts by ascending a non-hexatonic F dorian scale on the Fmi7, followed by what starts out like many of our typical descending altered dominant hexatonic lines. The Bb and Ab notes act as pivots because they're part of both the hexatonic line and the 5-to-3 device, so George simply continues with the device which resolves to the 3rd of Eb, the G, and then continues with a hexatonic line on Ebmaj7.

Joe Pass shows us more application of the 5-to-3 device in ex.2-22. On the first chord, Db7, Joe starts with what sounds like a typical Abmi7 hexatonic line. Jazz musicians frequently play lines that imply a II-V over just the V or over just the II. Then the line continues with a 5-to-3 device that goes from the 5th to the 3rd of a dom7 chord, the Db7, followed by an Ab minor triad going to a Db major triad. As the chord changes to C7, Joe again plays the 5-to-3 device on the dom7.

Ex.2-23A shows the 5-to-3 device as it would be used on Cmaj7 or C7, while ex.2-23B shows the 5-to-3 device adapted to chords with minor 3rds, in this case Cmi-maj7 or Cmi7. This variation will enable us to work out lines for a variety of situations.

Combining the descending chromatics with the 5-to-3 device

Ex.2-24 shows a combination that starts with a chromatic descent from the 7th to the 5th of a Cmaj7 chord. From this 5th it continues with a 5-to-3 device. From this 3rd the line follows the old "rule" of groups of two-note cells from Chapter 1, which allows the line to arrive back at a 7th, enabling a repeat of the whole thing an octave lower. The use of the 5-to-3 device means the line works great on Cmaj7, but might not be so good for Ami7 in many situations.

Ex.2-25 shows the same line as 2-24, but converted to Cmi-maj7 by flatting all the hexatonic E notes and using the 5-to-3 device for minor as shown in ex.2-23B. Unlike the major version, this minor combination still works on all the related chords (Ebmaj7#5, Ami9b5, F13#11, D13susb9, and B7alt).

Ex.2-26 combines various chromatics on a II-V-I line in C major. It starts with a chromatic descent from the 9th down to the 7th of Dmi7, then continues hexatonically. It reaches the b13th of G7alt, which is the 5th of the Abmi-maj7 hexatonic used for G7alt, so it continues with the 5-to-3 device for chords with minor 3rds. Again we use the two-note cell "rule" to get to the 5th of Cmaj7, beginning another 5-to-3 device in major to conclude the phrase.

Ex.2-27 shows a special combination on Cmaj7. It starts with an ascending Cmaj9 arpeggio. The top three notes of Cmaj9 are actually a G major triad, so we can use the 5-to-3 device in G major riding on top of Cmaj7. This brings us to B, the major 7th of C but also the 5th of the E minor triad that's contained in the Cmaj7, so we use the 5-to-3 device in E minor over the Cmaj7. This brings us to G, the actual 5th, starting the 5-to-3 device in C major. Now that we're on E we have one more trick. E is the 5th of the A minor triad found inside the C major hexatonic scale, so once again the 5-to-3 device in A minor is used to bring the line to a final resolution on the root.

I think that's enough of hexatonic-based lines for now, so let's move on.

Adding Chromatic Notes to Conventional Scale Patterns

Many method books for classical instrumentalists are filled with drills on diatonic patterns such as thirds and triads, and with patterns that add chromatics to the diatonic patterns, and usually many exercises based on the tonic triads of all keys embellished with various approach tones and combinations, usually involving chromatics. I think it's a good idea to check some of these out as they are so useful for jazz improvisation. I'm only going to do some of my favorites, but I'll suggest possible strings and fingerings so you can research more on your own if you wish (and you should). Perhaps the most complete sources designed for jazz players are Barry Finnerty's two books published by Sher Music Co., *The Serious Jazz Practice Book* and *The Serious Jazz Book II: The Harmonic Approach*. Let's start with some conventional seven-note scale patterns with added chromatics.

Look at ex.2-28. It's based on a simple pattern of ascending diatonic thirds going up and down one octave of the C major scale, but has a chromatic leading tone before the lower note of each third, making each cell three notes long. That's why they are usually written as triplets, but I like to play the three-note cells in 8th notes, shown in ex.2-29, which creates a more interesting polyrhythmic effect. I've heard Stan Getz, among many others, use this pattern in his improvisations.

Ex.2-30 shows a long three-octave fingering and "stringing" that uses the same fingerings in all three octaves, similar to what we did before. It's in C major but starts low on the instrument with a third starting from G with its chromatic leading tone F# and works its way up through three octave duplications of the same notes and fingerings (with some adjustments required due to the different tuning between the second and third strings) and then all the way back down. The fingerings are practical and playable, but if you hate them or find ones you prefer, please feel free. They are only suggestions.

You should also work the patterns out across the fingerboard in positions, and also, as I usually do when practicing, work them out full-range from the lowest notes on the guitar to the highest and all the way back down.

Ex.2-31 is the same thing in C melodic minor, but I'm only showing a "slice," the octave from C to "shining" C ascending and descending (the descending uses the same notes as the ascending making it the "jazz melodic minor," not the classical which descends using the same notes as the natural minor), but based on the same locations used in 2-30, so you should be able to work out the full range since the fingerings repeat in each octave duplication.

Ex.2-32 shows the the same pattern of chromaticised thirds transposed to the key of F major. Again it's a one-octave "slice" from F to F, but still in the same fingerboard regions to demonstrate some possible fingerings used for transposing. Your assignment is to transpose to all other keys.

Ex.2-33 is the same as 2-32, using the same key signature, but converted to F melodic minor by flatting the A notes.

In ex.2-34 we return to C major in the same regions, but with a modified pattern that starts on the lower diatonic note of each third, followed by the chromatic lower neighbor before returning to the starting note and skipping up the third. This creates a four-note cell which is then sequenced up the scale to start on each degree. Again this is a one-octave "slice," so it's up to you to work out the full range. I'm also leaving it up to you to convert it to melodic minor and to transpose to all other keys.

Ex.2-35 is actually the same as 2-34 but with a rhythmic displacement of one eighth-note that changes the perceived "shape" of the four-note cells. I've heard this variation in the playing of Hank Garland as well as Joe Pass.

The variation shown in ex.2-36 comes from Wes Montgomery and is in three-four time. It starts the same as 2-34, but after skipping up the third the upper note goes to *its* chromatic lower neighbor and back. We can extract a "rule": before going elsewhere a chromatic neighbor tone should be followed by its resolution tone, the note that it's the neighbor of.

(continued on next page)

Diatonic Triads and Seventh Chords with Added Chromatics

All the chromaticised diatonic patterns we've done so far are based on simple diatonic thirds. You could (and should) experiment with applying the same concepts to other diatonic intervals, such as fourths and fifths, but that will be up to you so I can move on to other things without running out of paper. Let's try some chromaticised patterns based on diatonic triads and on diatonic seventh chords.

First will be a demonstration of one way to play the straight diatonic triads going up the fingerboard along two strings. Ex.2-37 shows the basic pattern with strings and fingerings.

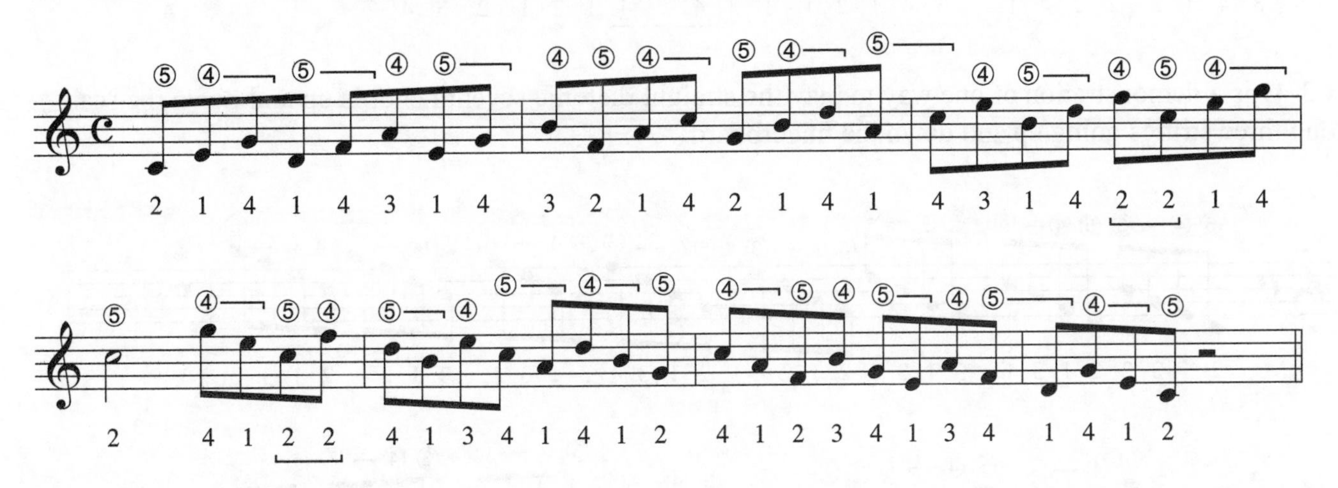

Ex.2-38 is a variation. The fingerings and strings aren't given because you can work them out using ex.2-37.

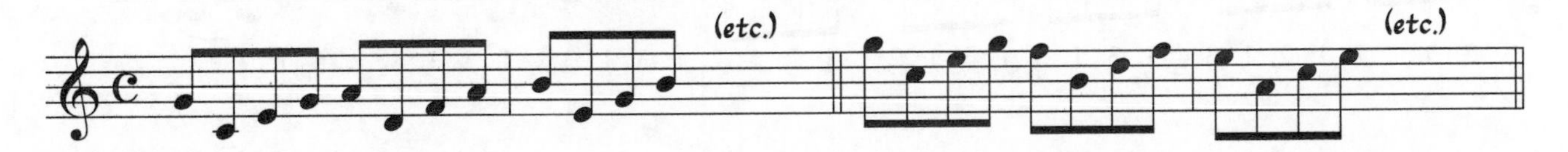

Ex.2-39 (on the following page) is a one-octave "slice" showing ascending triads with chromatic leading tones added before the first note (the root) of each triad, going up and down the scale. The strings and fingerings are from the same regions as the simple thirds examples. Work out the full range version using the octave duplication of fingerings, then transpose keys and convert to melodic minor. All this applies to the following examples as well.

Ex.2-40 shows the descending triads going up and down the scale with chromatic leading tones added before the first note (the fifth) of each triad.

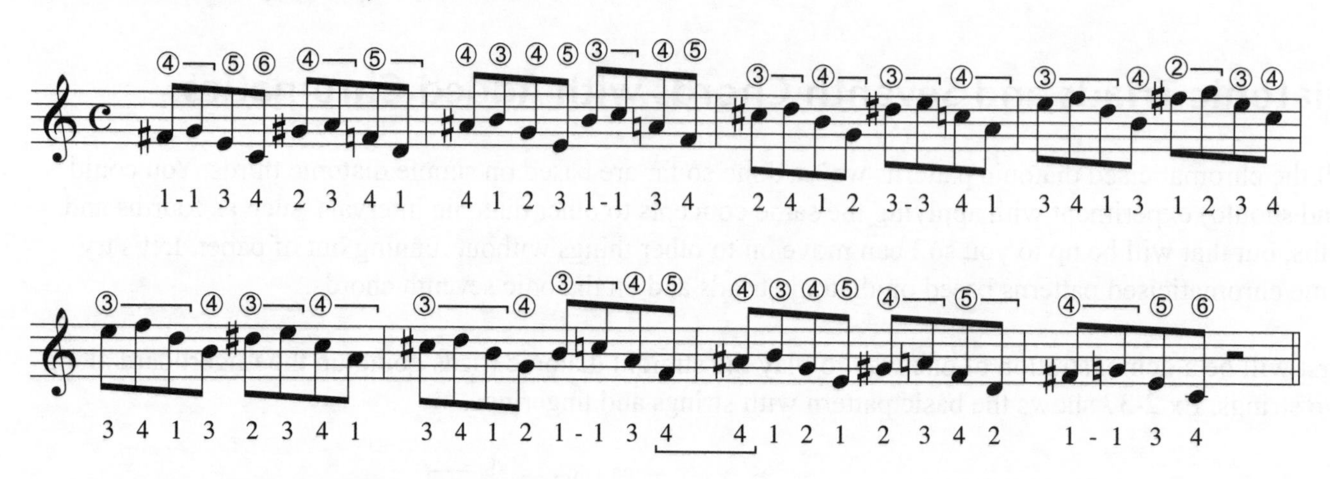

Ex.2-41 is a demonstration of one way to play the straight diatonic seventh chords up and down the scale along three strings going up and down the fingerboard.

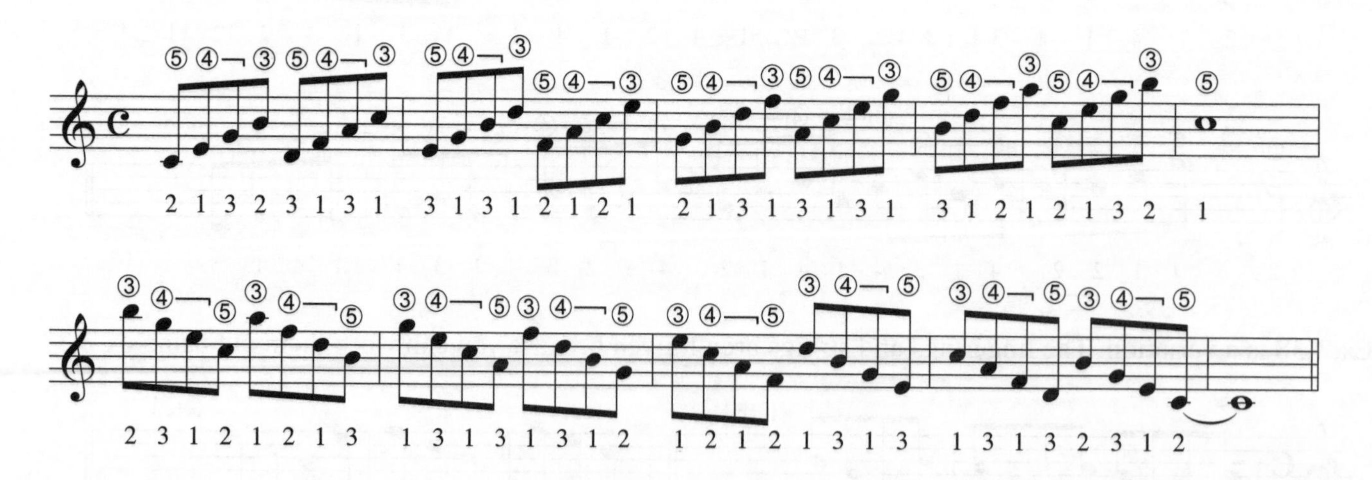

Ex.2-42 (on the next page) also comes from Wes Montgomery. It's based on the strings and fingerings given in ex.2-41. It's in three-four time and starts out like ex.2-36 but continues up the seventh chord, forming a six-note cell. Using this example as a model, work out the fingerings on all the other sets of three consecutive strings.

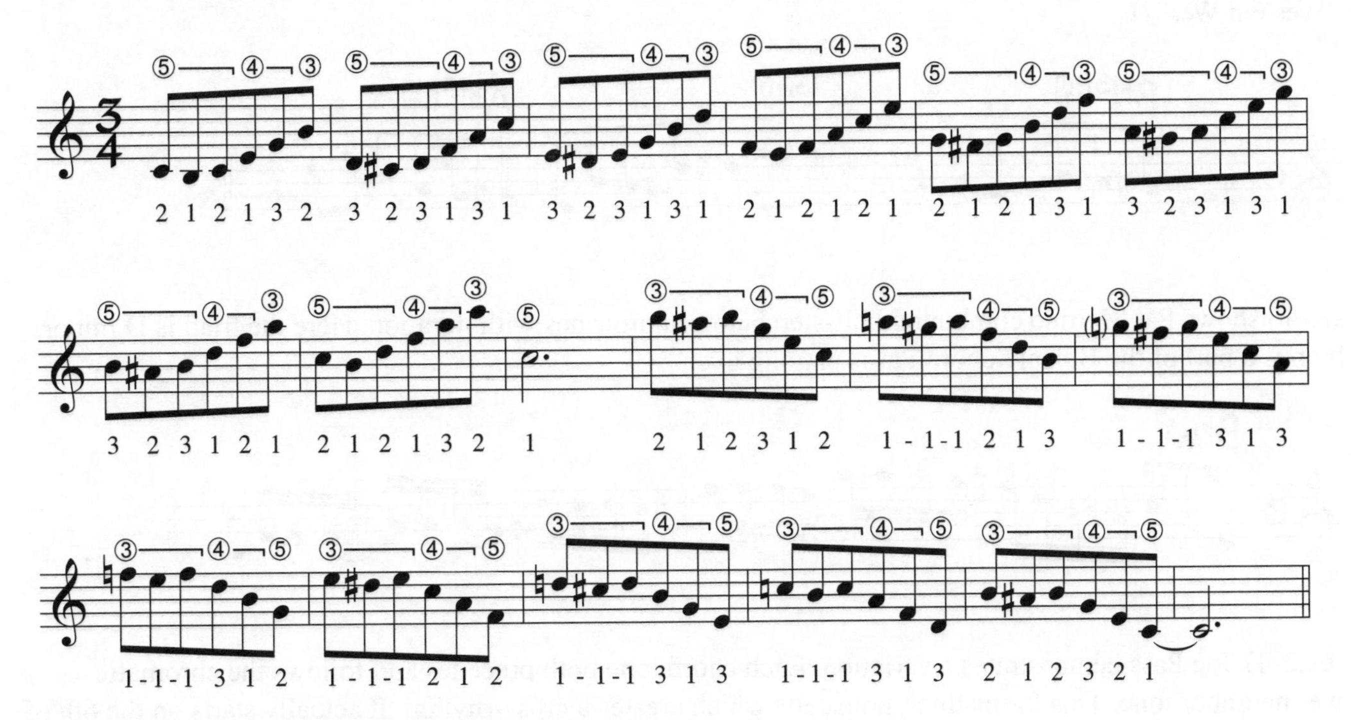

Using Added Chromatic Notes on Tonic Triads

The classical methods mentioned earlier generally recognize that only the notes from the tonic triad are stable enough to act as reliable targets for various chromatic approaches and approach combinations. In jazz we'll have much more leeway, but the principle is generally valid and most of the following studies will be based on that concept. First let's check out some actual recorded examples.

Actual recorded examples of chromatically embellished triads

Ex.2-43 has Wes showing us how we can make a line by approaching each note of the tonic triad, in this case a C major triad, from a half-step below.

Wes does it again in ex.2-44, but this time the tonic triad is a Bb minor triad.

Ex.2-45 shows Wes using the same device on several different triads in a row, but very adventurously on upper structure triads superimposed over different chords. First it's on a G major triad over Bb7, creating a Bb13b9 sound. Next it's a B major triad over A7, creating an A13#11, and finally an F major triad over Ab7, another 13b9 sound. This passage is actually a fragment from the bridge of Wes's composition "SOS" (or is it "Wes Oh Wes"?).

Ex.2-46 shows Pat Martino combining half-step below approaches with iteration. Here the triad is D minor, which is a part of the Bbmaj7 chord Pat is playing over.

In ex.2-47 Joe Pass demonstrates a variation. Each chord tone both precedes and follows the chromatic lower neighbor tone. This forms three-note cells which creates a cross-rhythm. It actually starts on the 6th of the Db chord, but could be thought of as an overlap of a Bb minor triad and a Db major triad.

Ex.2-48 is actually from saxophonist Charlie Parker. You will hear all the patterns in this book all over the playing of saxophonists, trumpeters, and pianists among others. This a line from a "Rhythm Changes" tune. When I first heard it I just had to find out what it was, so after transcribing it I knew I had to study chromatically enhanced triads. The notes of the triad occur "out of order" and are alternately approached from a half-step below and a diatonic scale step above (as is usual in most of the classical exercises). Notice that Parker continues to embellish the tonic Bb major triad right across the other chord changes, the Cmi7 and the F7.

Ex.2-49 shows Joe Pass using "enclosures," starting on the scale step above, then going straight to the half-step below before resolving to the chord tone. In this example Joe is only using the root and the 5th of the tonic triad, C major.

Ex.2-50, Joe again, using the root and third of an E minor triad to imply G6. Here he starts on the scale step above, but this time passes through the chord tone on the way down to the chromatic lower neighbor, of course resolving before moving on.

In ex.2-51 Joe does the same thing as in 2-50 but on the pure tonic triad notes.

The "Mona Lisa" and "Solar" licks

Joe introduces a new idea in ex.2-52. He starts by reversing the earlier enclosure order, placing the lower neighbor first followed by the upper, then resolution. This is followed by the next chord tone, forming a four-note cell, then the reversed enclosure on that chord tone, etc. This ordering of notes can be placed two different ways rhythmically. Let's analyze.

Ex.2-53 shows a rhythmic displacement of the last example transposed to the key of C. I sometimes call this the "Mona Lisa lick" since it resembles melodic embellishments used in that melody.

Ex.2-54 is rhythmically placed like 2-52, but transposed to the key of C. I sometimes call this the "Solar lick" since it resembles melodic embellishments used in that melody. Of course Solar is in C minor and uses rhythmic anticipations so it's not a steady string of eighth-notes.

Practicing the Chromatically Embellished Triads

Ex.2-55 (on the following page) shows a user-friendly Bb major-triad arpeggio form and fingering that spans three octaves with the fingerings duplicated in each octave. Let's use this form on the fingerboard to practice exercises to develop fluency with the chromatically embellished triads.

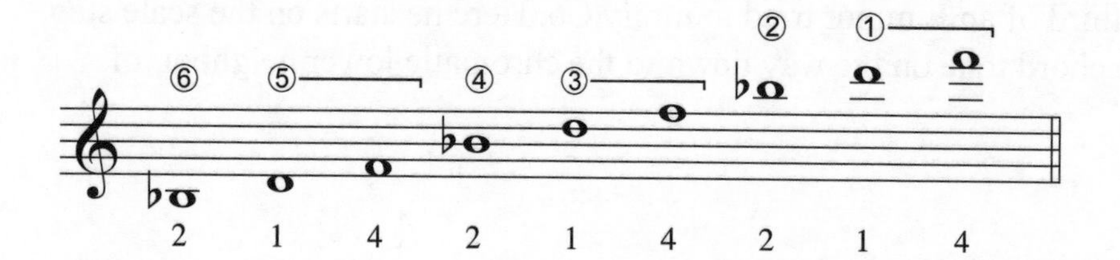

Approaching chord tones from a half-step below

Ex.2-56 shows a pattern that approaches each chord tone from a half-step below, going all the way up and back down with the strings and fingerings shown.

Ex.2-57 shows the same thing rhythmically displaced by one-eighth note with slurs added (use hammer-ons). The strings and fingerings are the same as in 2-56, so the example only shows enough to get you started. Continue all the way up and back down.

Ex.2-58 shows a 16th note variation that uses four-note cells and the same slurs, strings, and fingerings.

Ex.2-59 has the bottom note of each triad inversion approached from a half-step below going up, and the top note of each descending triad inversion approached from a half-step below going down. The strings and fingerings are shown.

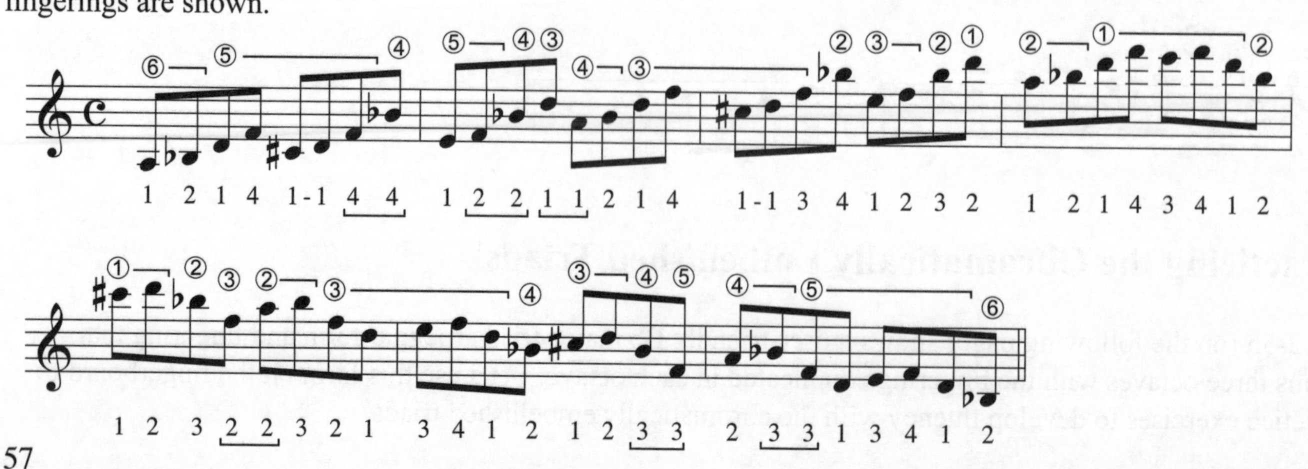

Ex.2-60 shows the same thing rhythmically displaced by one eighth-note with slurs added. The strings and fingerings are the same as in 2-59. Continue all the way up and back.

Ex.2-61 is derived from 2-59 by leaving out the third note from each four-note cell, changing them into three-note cells. The strings and fingerings are given.

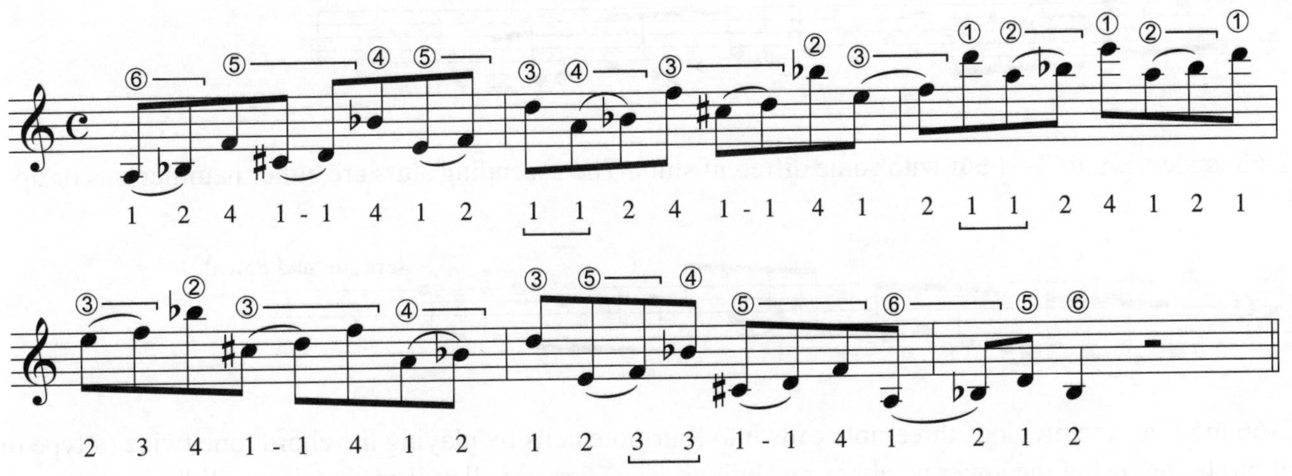

Adding diatonic upper neighbor tones

Ex.2-62 shows a combination that, in addition to using chromatic lower neighbors, also introduces diatonic upper neighbor tones. The chord tones occur out of order with alternating lower and upper neighbor tones.

Ex.2-63 uses the same strings and fingerings as 2-62 but is rhythmically displaced by one eighth-note with slurs added. Continue all the way up and back down.

Starting on the chord tones and using chromatic lower neighbors

Ex.2-64 creates three-note cells by starting with each chord tone before using the chromatic lower neighbor to return the same chord tone. Work out the strings and fingerings based on the preceding examples. Notice the slurs. They are all pull-offs or down-slides.

Ex.2-65 is identical to 2-64 but with some different slurs. The ascending slurs are either hammer-ons or up-slides.

Ex.2-66 modifies the previous three-note cells into four-note cells by playing the chord tone twice (a type of iteration) before using the lower neighbor resolutions. The slurs are all pull-offs or down-slides.

Ex.2-67 changes the three-note cells into four-note cells using a different method, adding a skipped-to chord tone after each three-note cell. Work out the strings and fingerings (hint: you can use the same strings and fingers for the same notes as found in ex.2-61).

Ex.2-68 is a rhythmic displacement of 2-67 with different slurs. Continue all the way up and back down.

A classic three-note cell

Ex.2-69 shows a new combination. It uses both the diatonic upper neighbor tone and the chromatic lower neighbor tone before resolving into each chord tone. Each cell is three notes long, two eighths followed by a quarter. All three notes in each cell are played on the same string, so after the first three cells the strings and fingerings to go all the way up and down should be obvious.

Ex.2-70 has the same notes as 2-69, but the strings and fingerings are different so the example shows them going all the way up. Once you start descending you will know what to do.

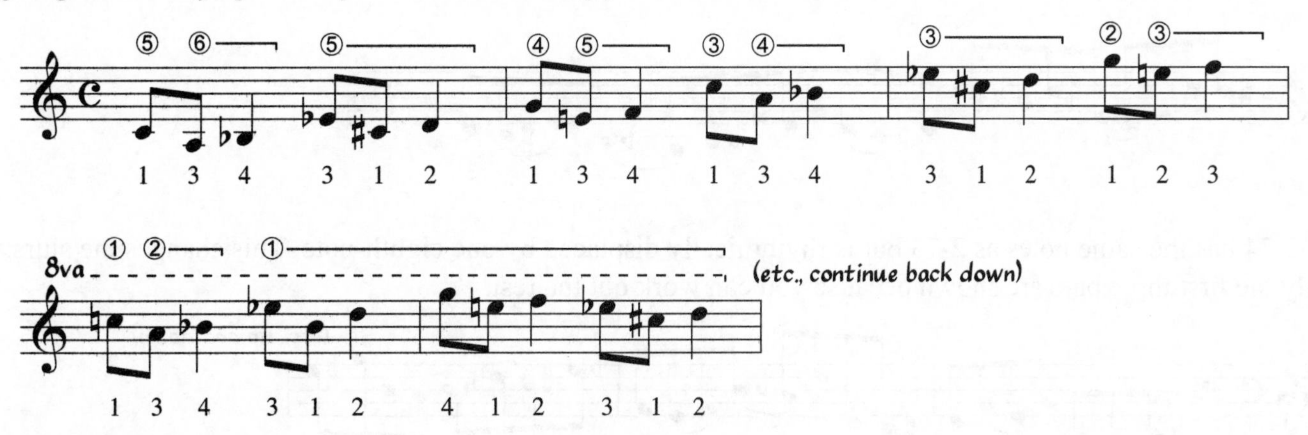

Ex.2-71 also has the same notes grouped in three-note cells, but the rhythm is all eighth-notes. You can use the strings and fingerings from both ex.2-69 and ex.2-70.

More variations

Ex.2-72 changes the three-note cells into four-note cells by adding a skipped-to chord tone after each three-note cell. The strings and fingerings are given.

Ex.2-73 shows a combination using a three-note cell from 2-65 which skips a chord tone and is followed by a three-note cell from 2-70. Then it returns to the skipped chord tone and repeats the process. The entire ascending and descending exercise is shown, but you can work out the strings and fingerings.

Ex.2-74 has the same notes as 2-73 but is rhythmically displaced by one eighth-note. This changes the slurs. Only the first three bars are shown because you can work out the rest.

In ex.2-75 the second three-note cell has been modified into a five-note cell by passing through the chord tone on the way down to the lower neighbor, then skipping back up to the upper neighbor before returning to the chord tone. The three-note and five-note cells alternate to produce eight-note cells. I'm leaving it up to you to find the strings and fingerings and to continue all the way up and back down.

Ex.2-76 shows the second three-note cell converted into a five-note cell through a different process. Each five-note cell starts a whole-step above each chord tone, followed by the chord tone which is followed by a chromatic enclosure (a half-step above to a half-step below) resolving to each chord tone. I've shown enough of the ascending and descending portions of the exercise with strings and fingerings so you can work out the whole thing.

(continued on next page)

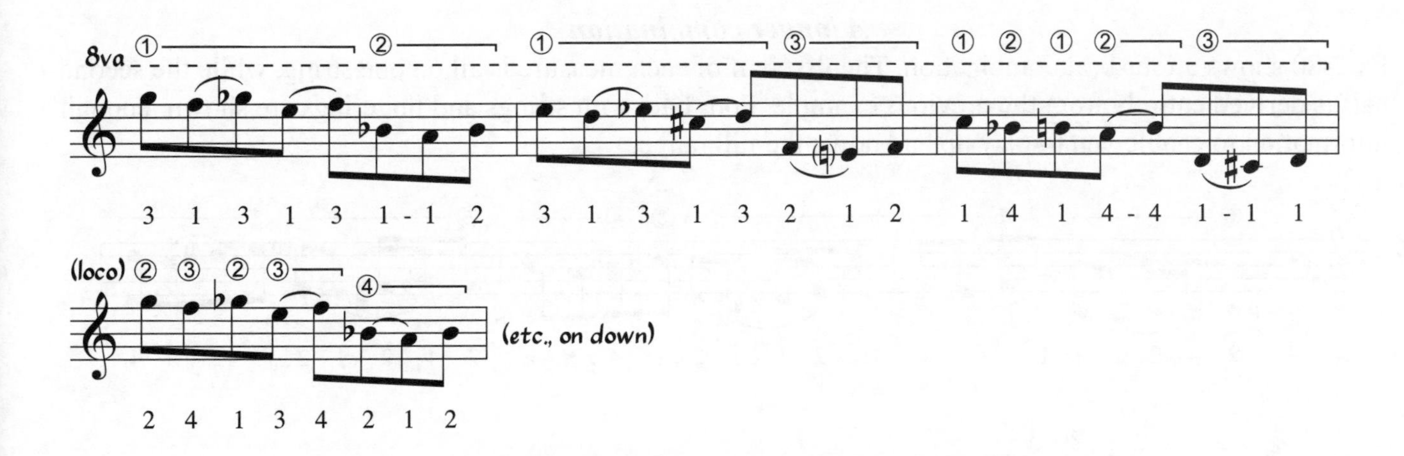

Using the chromatic "wind-up"

In ex.2-77 the first three-note cell from 2-74 is converted into a five-note cell by using a chromatic "wind-up." It begins with the first chord tone as a pick-up note, followed by a half-step up, then a repeat of the chord tone to a half-step below and back before moving on to the original three-note second cell. Three measures are shown to get you started.

A classic four-note cell

Ex.2-78 is a classic combination using the upper neighbor-chord tone-lower neighbor-chord tone sequence to generate four-note cells. In this example all four notes of each cell are played on the same string so only the first three cells need to be shown. Play up and down the full range.

Ex.2-79 shows the same combination using alternate strings and fingerings. The first three bars are shown to give enough information to enable you to complete the full-range exercise.

A longer combination

Ex.2-80 shows a four-beat combination. The first half of each measure is all on one string, while the second half is derived entirely from the previous example. Four bars with strings and fingerings are shown, enough information to enable you to play up and down the full range.

The "Mona Lisa" and "Solar" licks again

Ex.2-81 shows the strings and fingerings for the first two bars of what I called the "Mona Lisa lick" above. Complete the full-range exercise.

For ex.2-82 use the same strings and fingerings as used in 2-81, but with the rhythmic displacement and slurs as shown. This results in what I called the "Solar lick" above. Play up and down the full range.

Patterns using double-approaches

Now let's take a look at some patterns that use double-approaches where there's either two approach notes below in combination with one from above, or two approach notes above in combination with one from below.

Ex.2-83 (on the next page) uses two approach notes below in combination with one from above when ascending, and two approach notes above in combination with one from below when descending. When ascending, the final enclosure before each chord tone is always a minor 3rd and the upper enclosure tone is always a diatonic upper neighbor. This results in the lower enclosure tone of the major 3rd being a whole-step below rather than a half-step as in all the previous examples. However, *it* is approached with a lower chromatic approach tone. When descending, it's business as usual. Since we've entered new territory the entire exercise is shown with strings and fingerings.

Ex.2-84 uses two approach notes above in combination with one from below when ascending, and two approach notes below in combination with one from above when descending. The entire exercise is shown with strings and fingerings.

Ex.2-85 alternates between the double-approaches from 2-83 and 2-84, starting with 2-83. Use the strings and fingerings from the previous examples and play up and down the full range.

Ex.2-86 alternates between the double-approaches from 2-83 and 2-84, starting with 2-84. You know what to do.

Patterns using elaborated minor-third enclosures

These next patterns will use chromatically filled-in minor-thirds followed by some regular approach-tone combinations.

Ex.2-87 starts with an ascending chromatic triplet filling-in a minor-third surrounding the chord tone before skipping back to the lower neighbor, then resolving. This is then combined with a familiar pattern before repeating at the next chord tone. The first three bars with strings and fingerings are shown ascending and the first bar with strings and fingerings are shown descending to get you started.

Ex.2-88 reverses the direction of the elaborated minor-third enclosures, showing the first two bars ascending and the first two descending.

A pattern using double-approaches from both below and above

Ex.2-89 (on the following page) is a pattern which starts a whole-step below each chord tone and climbs to a half-step below before skipping up to a whole-step above and descending chromatically to the target note. It's combined with the familiar pattern used before. The entire ascending notation with strings and fingerings are shown along with enough of the descending portion so you can work it out.

Embellished triad wrap-up

In order to wrap-up the embellished triads, we need to address the issue of minor triads and of transposing the patterns into other keys.

Ex.2-90 shows a user-friendly Bb minor-triad arpeggio form and fingering that spans three octaves with the fingerings duplicated in each octave. Let's use this form on the fingerboard to practice exercises to develop fluency with the chromatically embellished minor triads. I'm not going to show all the exercises converted to minor. In fact I'm only going to show part of one. It is your homework assignment to work out all of the patterns in minor.

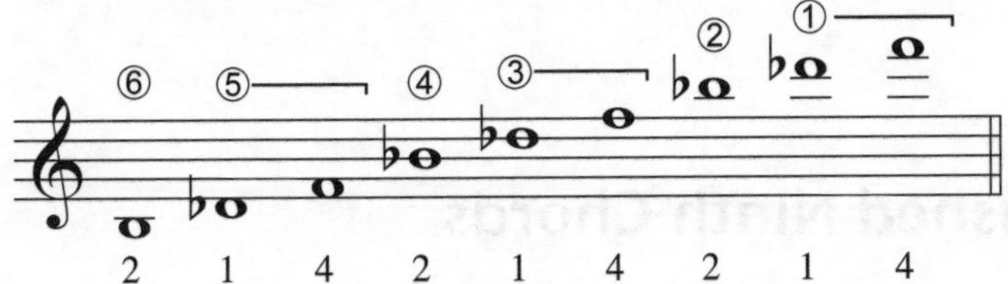

Ex.2-91 shows a pattern based on 2-76 converted to minor. I've shown enough so you can work out the rest.

Ex.2-92 shows a user-friendly first-inversion F major-triad arpeggio form and fingering that spans three octaves with the fingerings duplicated in each octave. This we can use to aid in working out the transpositions of the patterns to all keys.

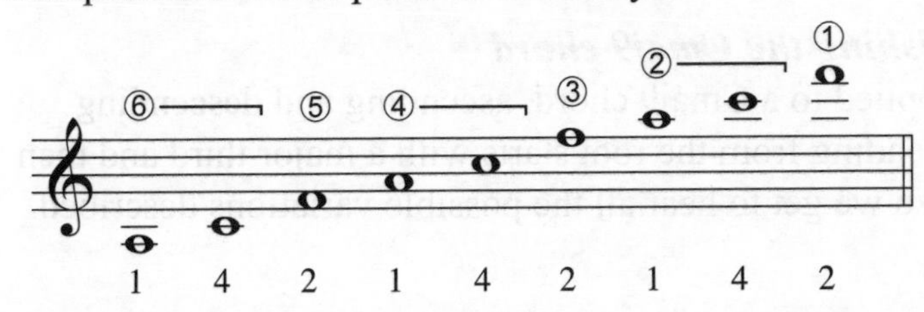

Ex.2-93 uses the F major-triad arpeggio to play a pattern based on 2-62. You should be able to work out the entire full-range exercise. Again, I'm only going to show part of one pattern, so you know what to do.

Ex.2-94 shows a user-friendly first-inversion F minor-triad arpeggio form and fingering that spans three octaves with the fingerings duplicated in each octave.

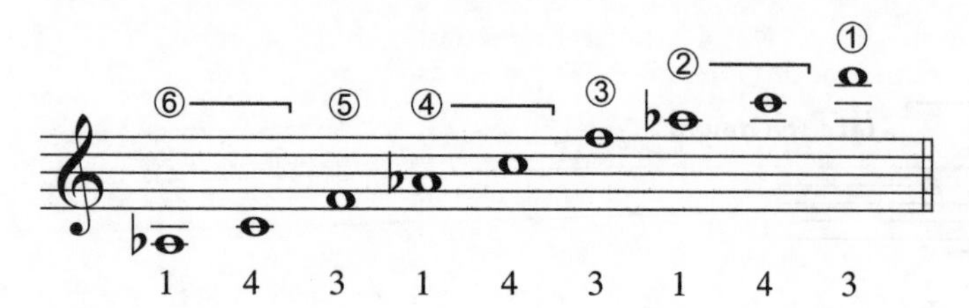

Ex.2-95 shows a portion of a minor-triad pattern based on 2-79.

Embellishing triads could go on and on, but I think we'll stop for now so we can explore some chromatically embellished ninth chords.

Exercises on Chromatically Embellished Ninth Chords

Let's start with the idea that, rather than using some conventional modal chord scale, we can improvise lines over various kinds of ninth chords using the chromatic scale on all of them. The idea will prove good if we can get the chord tones to land on the strong beats (beats one and three in four-four time – for a compete explanation I again refer you to *The Serious Jazz Book II – The Harmonic Approach* by Barry Finnerty). If we start with a chord tone on a strong beat and the next chord tone is a major third above or below, we can simply go chromatically up or down, respectively, in eighth-notes and we'll arrive at that next chord tone on the next strong beat. If the next chord tone is a minor third above, we can ascend chromatically to the half-step below, then skip up to the diatonic scale tone above before arriving at the target on the strong beat. If we're going a minor third below, we descend chromatically to the half-step above, then skip to a half-step below before resolving on the strong beat. Let's put it to the test.

Chromatically embellishing the Cmaj9 chord

Ex.2-96 (on the following page) shows the concept applied to a Cmaj9 chord, ascending and descending with strings and fingerings given. The maj9 chord ascending from the root starts with a major third and then alternates minor and major thirds up and back down, so we get to hear all the possible variations described in the previous paragraph.

Perhaps you noticed that the minor thirds resulted in slightly more interesting melodies due to the skips and changes in direction. Well, we don't have to ascend and descend chromatically all the way on major thirds. Using ideas derived from earlier studies we can mimic those melodic shapes on our major thirds, too.

Ex.2-97 shows one possible version.

Ex.2-98 is the same ascending, but uses shapes derived from ex.2-27 (what I called the "5-to-3 device") when descending.

Ex.2-99 introduces some angularity by leaping up to a descending approach idea when ascending and vice-versa.

Ex.2-100 goes up the Cmaj9 arpeggio and then follows a pattern using chromatic enclosures and skips.

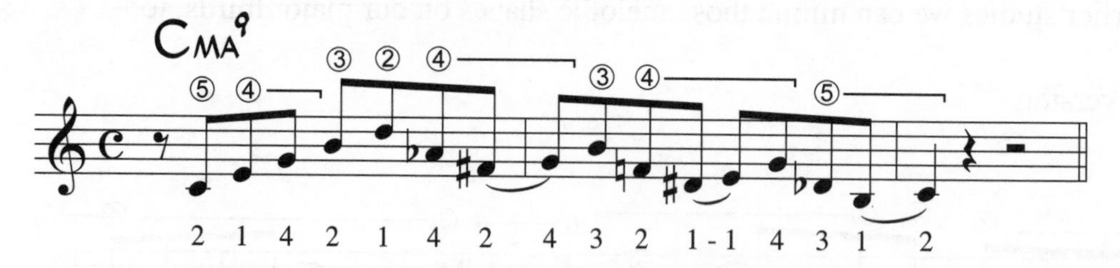

Ex.2-101 goes up the Cmaj9 arpeggio and then follows a pattern using skips and double-approaches from above.

Chromatically embellishing the C9 chord

Now let's change the chord quality from major to dominant. We'll apply the same chromatic embellishments to C9 that we did to Cmaj9. The only difference is Bb replacing B natural, so now we have one major third followed by two minor-thirds in a row, then another major third.

Ex.2-102 is the C9 arpeggio with the thirds filled-in with all the chromatics. It's shown ascending and descending with strings and fingerings given.

Ex.2-103 is based on 2-91 converted to C9.

Ex.2-104 is based on 2-92 converted to C9. It only borrows one shape derived from ex.2-27 ("5-to-3") when descending because the b7th makes it unusable at that degree.

Ex.2-105 is based on 2-93 converted to C9.

Ex.2-106 goes up the C9 arpeggio and then follows a pattern using chromatic enclosures and skips.

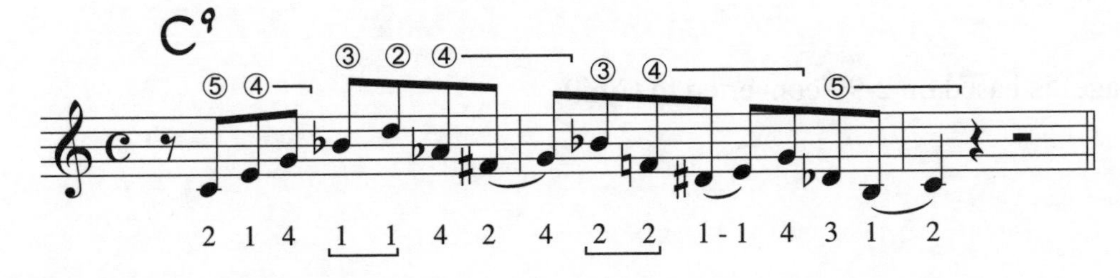

Ex.2-107 goes up the C9 arpeggio and then follows a pattern using skips and double-approaches from above.

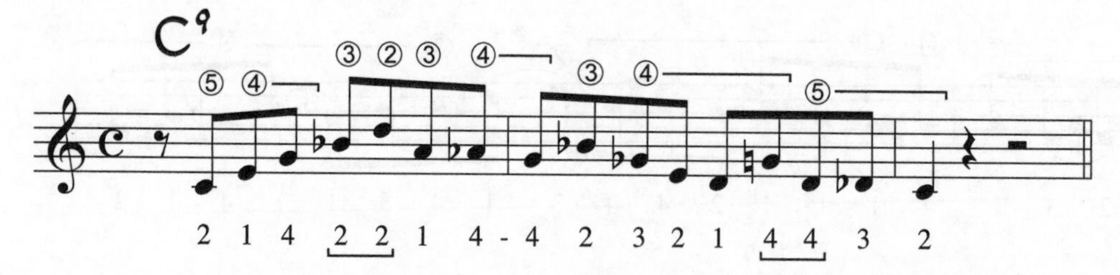

Chromatically embellishing the Cmi9 chord

Next we'll change the chord quality from dominant to mi9. We'll apply the same chromatic embellishments to Cmi9 that we did to C9 (except for the "5-to-3" from 2-27, which doesn't really work on the mi9 chord). Changing the E to Eb results in alternating minor and major thirds again, but starting with the minor-third this time.

Ex.2-108 is the Cmi9 arpeggio with the thirds filled-in with all the chromatics. It's shown ascending and descending with strings and fingerings given.

Ex.2-109 is based on 2-97 converted to Cmi9.

Ex.2-110 (on the following page) is based on 2-99 converted to Cmi9.

Ex.2-111 goes up the Cmi9 arpeggio and follows the pattern using chromatic enclosures and skips.

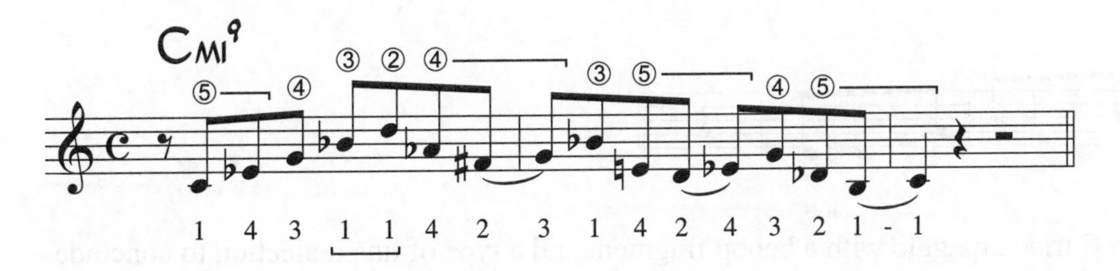

Ex.2-112 goes up the Cmi9 arpeggio and follows the pattern using skips and double-approaches from above.

Ninth chord wrap-up

We've only done three kinds of ninth chords in one key and in one region of the fingerboard, but I'm going to wrap it up here so we can get to the wealth of information to come. That means some serious homework for you. Use these examples as models to play the studies in all keys and on different string groupings. You should also try other ninth chord types that are composed of all major and minor thirds, such as mi-maj9 and mi9b5. Also remember that all the given strings and fingerings are practical suggestions only (although the "stringing" was carefully chosen to get the maximum amount of slurs appropriate for jazz phrasing). Feel free to experiment and use the fingerings that work best for you. All the slurs are optional and each study should be practiced both with and without the slurs.

Before we move on I'd like to mention a closely related concept, using chromatic scales to imply whole-tone augmented sounds and diminished-dom7b9 sounds. If you ascend or descend a chromatic scale in eighth-notes (or sixteenth-notes) you imply a whole-tone scale on the beats and an augmented triad on the strong beats. If you ascend or descend a chromatic scale in triplets you outline a diminished 7th chord, and starting on the 3rd, 5th, b7th, or b9th of a dominant-type chord outlines those chord tones.

Introducing the "Bebop Scales"

Some actual recorded examples

Play ex.2-113, showing Joe Pass using what is now frequently called a "bebop dominant scale" in combination with a Bbmaj7 arpeggio at the beginning and a chromatic enclosure at the end.

Ex.2-114 shows Joe going down the bebop scale using the Bbmaj7 arpeggio from the Bb note and followed by the old 5-to-3 device.

In ex.2-115 Joe follows a C triad arpeggio with a bebop fragment and a type of line deflection to conclude.

Ex.2-116 starts by ascending an Emi7b5 arpeggio, which is 3-5-b7-9 of C9. Then Joe uses the double-approach from both below and above the 7th, then continues descending the bebop scale.

You can analyze the details of ex.2-117 showing Joe combining the bebop scale with deflections and chromatic enclosures.

Before showing more beautiful examples of bebop scales being used by jazz guitar masters, I think we need to define and analyze just what bebop scales are.

Bebop scales defined and analyzed

A bebop scale is an eight-note scale derived from a standard seven-note scale by adding one chromatic note. The added-note is chosen in order to align chord tones in the scale with the beats, and to place any tricky "avoid" notes off the beats. In order to more clearly understand how this works and how it was actually used in the bebop era, we'll have to review a tiny bit of music theory. Since the Joe Pass examples shown above were all on C7, the dominant of F major, let's use the key of F major for our analysis.

Ex.2-118 shows the diatonic seventh chords for the key of F major. Three of the chords, Fmaj7 (the I), Ami7 (the III), and Dmi7 (the VI), are labeled as resolution chords. None of these chords contain the note Bb, which is the avoid note for F major, so they can function as points of resolution for chord progressions in F major. The other four chords, Gmi7 (the II), Bbmaj7 (the IV), C7 (the V), and Emi7b5 (the VII), are labeled as tension chords. They all contain the note Bb and don't sound resolved in F major, so they are used to create or maintain tension in the key of F.

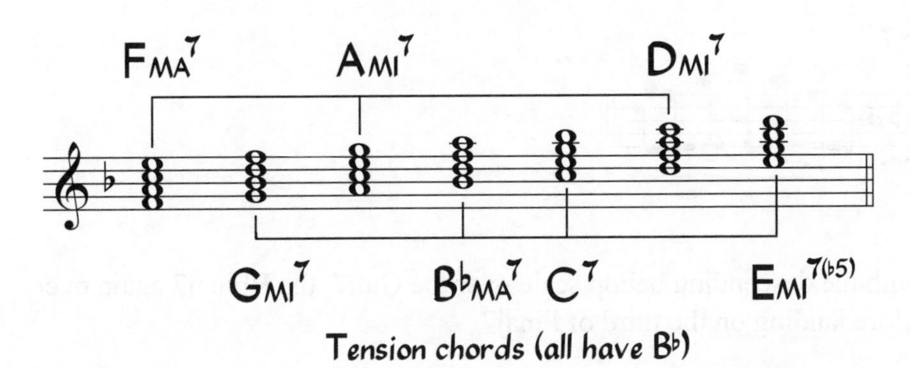

If you play up an F major scale in eighth-notes over an Fmaj7 chord, for the first measure all is well because the chord tones fall on the beats and the avoid note, Bb, is off the beat surrounded by on-the-beat chord tones. If you descend the F major scale in eighth-notes over the Fmaj7 chord, however, all is not well because now the on-the-beat chord tones spell-out a Gmi7 chord. Bb is on the beat so the line clashes with the Fmaj7 chord (and also with the Ami7 and Dmi7 chords).

Ex.2-119 shows a solution discovered by the beboppers. When descending from the F they added an off-beat chromatic note between the sixth and the fifth. This places the fifth back on the beat and moves the Bb back to the off-beat, making it a passing tone between two strong on-the-beat chord tones. This produces what is commonly called the "F bebop major scale", and in the key of F major it can be used over Fmaj7, Ami7, and Dmi7.

For the C7 chord (and the other tension chords as well), the problem is reversed. Now we want the Bb to land on the beat. Descending from the note C this is accomplished by adding the B natural on the off-beat, which moves the Bb back on the beat.

Ex.2-120 shows the result, commonly called the "C bebop dominant scale," and in the key of F major it can be used over Gmi7, Bbmaj7, C7, and Emi7b5. This means that the C bebop dominant scale can be used over unaltered II-V progressions since both Gmi7 (the II) and C7 (the V) are both tension chords. This is why the beboppers played like the II and the V were really just one sound. Let's check it out.

C Bebop Dominant Scale:

GMI7, B♭MA7, C7, EMI7(♭5)

Actual examples of bebop dominant scales used on II chords and II-V progressions

Ex.2-121 shows Joe Pass using the C bebop dominant scale over Gmi7 and a device over the C7 that was also favored by Wes Montgomery, the Bbmaj9 arpeggio.

Ex.2-122, also from Joe Pass, starts with the descending bebop scale over the Gmi7, the Bbmaj7 again over C7, followed by a C7b13 arpeggio before landing on the third of Fmaj7.

By now perhaps you're wondering if Joe Pass is the only person to do this. Let's find out if Pat Martino agrees with Joe.

Ex.2-123 shows a line played by Pat Martino over a Gmi7 chord using the C bebop dominant scale.

Ex.2-124 is another line from Pat over a Gmi7 chord using the C bebop dominant scale.

Ex.2-125 shows Pat Martino doing it again.

Does Wes Montgomery agree with Joe and Pat?

Ex.2-126 shows Wes Montgomery using a bebop fragment over C7.

Ex.2-127 shows Wes Montgomery using a bebop fragment over Gmi7 going to C7.

Does Tal Farlow agree with Joe and Pat and Wes?

Ex.2-128 is from Tal Farlow. I'll leave the analysis up to you.

Ex.2-129 is one more from Tal.

Actual examples of bebop major scales used on I chords and V-I progressions

Ex.2-130, from Joe Pass, is a typical bebop major line over Fmaj7.

Ex.2-131, also from Joe Pass, was actually played over C7 to Fmaj7. The chord symbol Fmaj7 indicates the use of the F bebop major scale over the V-I progression, an example of harmonic anticipation.

Ex.2-132 shows Wes Montgomery using the F bebop major scale.

Ex.2-133 is a combination from Jimmy Raney using the F bebop major scale with a 5-to-3 device and a hexatonic fragment with a double-approach to the root from above.

Bebop Dominant Scale Exercises

Now it's time we get to some exercises to use the bebop scales to help develop fluency in the jazz language. These exercises will use forms and fingerings that span three octaves with the fingerings duplicated in each octave. In order to make the "swinging" slurs work, the "stringing" and fingerings ascend one way and descend another way. The next example will illustrate.

Ex.2-134 shows a C bebop dominant scale. It starts on a low G on the sixth string and uses strings and fingerings duplicated in each octave ascending and slightly modified strings and fingerings duplicated in each octave descending.

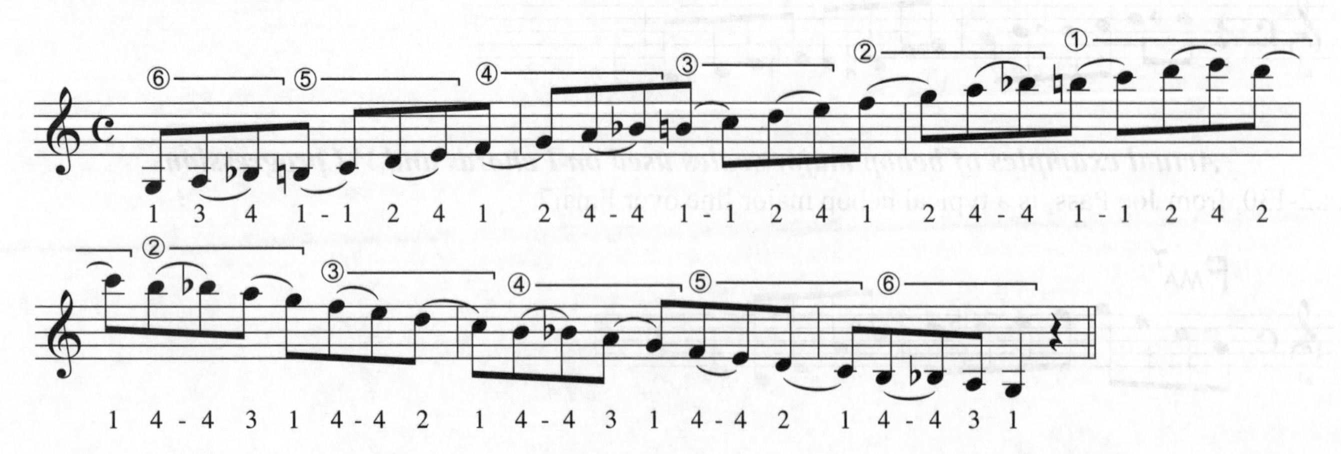

Exercises using the bebop dominant scale to develop vocabulary for improvisation

Ex.2-135 shows a C bebop dominant scale in combination with a Bbmaj9 arpeggio, using the arpeggio to ascend and the scale to descend. Since it begins and ends on the same note, it can easily be converted into a practice loop.

Ex.2-136 is a descending line based on the C bebop dominant scale. When the line reaches the 5th of C7, the note G, it uses a lower-upper neighbor tone combination followed by the old 5-to-3 device, and a chromatic enclosure of the root before continuing. At the bottom of the scale is shown the beginning of the ascending Bbmaj9 arpeggio as used in the previous example. Continue the line back to the starting note and create another practice loop if you wish.

Ex.2-137 shows another variation. As the line first reaches the 7th of C7, the note Bb, it skips up to D before continuing. This deflection causes the 5th, G, to fall on the off-beat, so we use a modified lower-upper neighbor tone combination that returns the G to the on-beat. Next is introduced a new variation on the 5-to-3 device, a "sawtooth" shaped melody. The chromatic enclosure of the root is the same as in the previous example. You can continue the line with the same ascending Bbmaj9 arpeggio to create a practice loop.

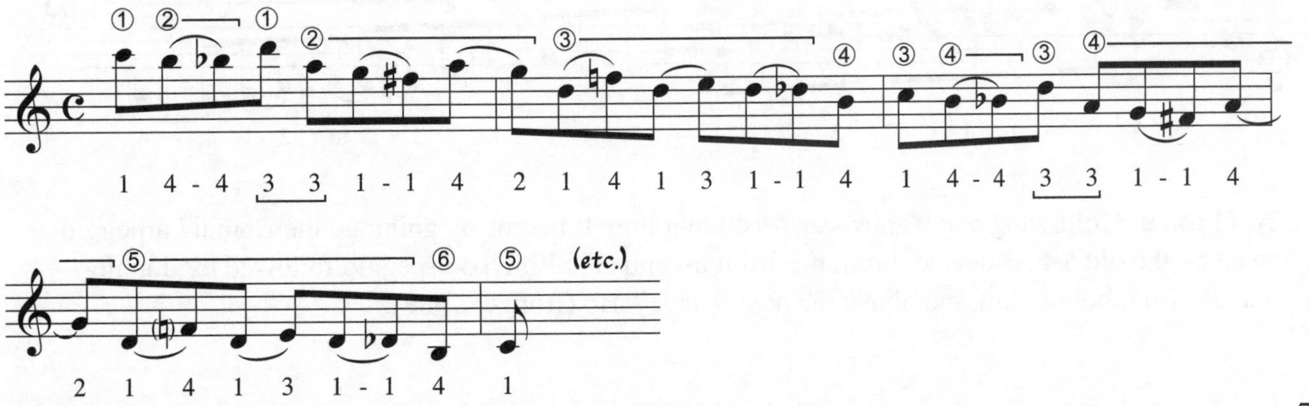

Ex.2-138 is yet another variation. I'll leave the analysis up to you this time.

Ex.2-139 starts with an ascending Bbmaj7 arpeggio, but using octave displacement to make the line descend. It's combined with the old 5-to-3 device.

Ex.2-140 is a variation based on 2-139. The 3rd of the Bbmaj7, D, skips directly to the 7th of Bbmaj7, the A, and then descends chromatically to the G.

Ex.2-141 shows a variation of 2-140. The Bb skips down to F#, the lower neighbor of G, before continuing as in the previous example.

Ex.2-142 introduces another twist, a double-approach from below the G target note followed by a single diatonic upper neighbor.

Ex.2-143 (on the following page) shows an ascending line. It begins by going up the Bbmaj7 arpeggio followed by the old 5-to-3 device. From the 3rd it ascends the Emi7b5 arpeggio followed by double-approaches from both below and above the next octave's Bb (from ex.2-89).

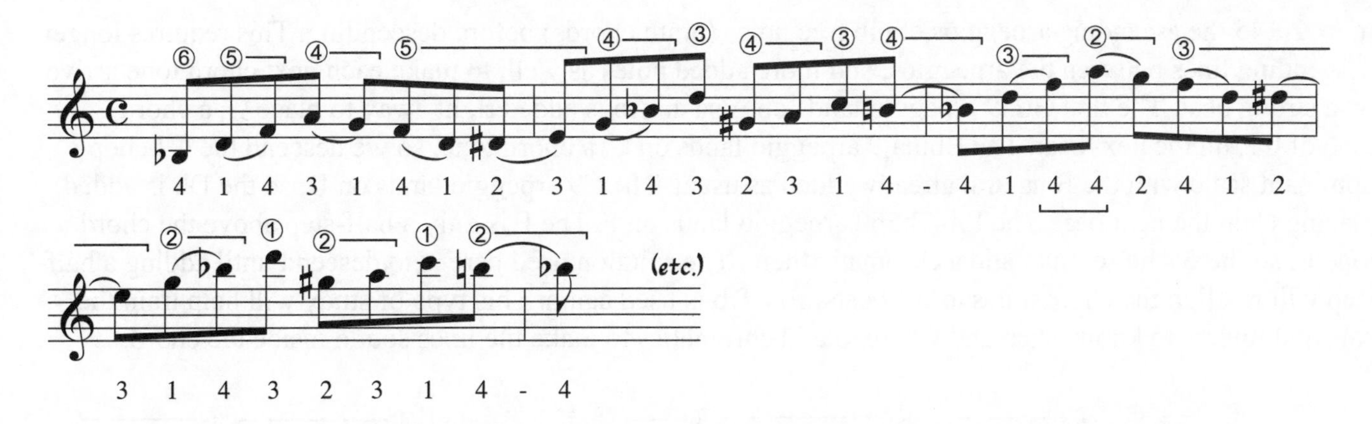

Exercises combining ascending arpeggios with descending bebop lines

The last example not only had the frequently used Bbmaj7 arpeggio, but also the Emi7b5 arpeggio, which in the context of C7 can be seen to be a 3-5-b7-9 arpeggio. If you look back at ex.2-118 you'll see that both Bbmaj7 and Emi7b5 are tension chords in the key of F. We can actually create more vocabulary-building exercises by combining ascending arpeggios of all four tension chords from ex.2-118 with various descending bebop lines. Let's check some out.

Ex.2-144 is an exercise starting with an ascending Gmi7 arpeggio followed by a descending bebop scale fragment that descends to Bb. From there it goes up the Bbmaj7 and descends scale-wise to C. After ascending the C7 arpeggio the descending bebop line has an added Ab note to make the C7 chord tones land on the beat. This brings us to the Emi7b5 arpeggio and a descending bebop scale to G, where the entire sequence is repeated in the next octave. Perhaps you noticed that the root notes of the four tension chords spell out the chord tones of the basic C7 chord. After the line reaches its upper limit it descends by using longer descending lines between the still ascending arpeggios. Enough is shown so you can work out the rest.

In ex.2-145 the ascending arpeggios climb five notes (ninth chords) before descending. This requires longer descending lines between the arpeggios, and more added notes as well, to make each next chord tone arrive on a strong beat. The first Gmi9 arpeggio lands on A so an Ab is added right away to place G, a chord tone of C7, on the next beat. The Bbmaj9 arpeggio lands on C, a chord tone, so we descend the C bebop dominant scale with the B natural already added as usual. The C9 arpeggio lands on D, so the Db is added placing C on the next beat. The Emi7b5b9 arpeggio lands on F. The F is only a half-step above the chord tone E, so there's no room to add a chromatic there. The solution used here is to descend until adding a half-step will re-align the chord tones to the beats, so a Db is used again. This type of study will help train the ears and fingers to know when and where to add chromatics to make the lines sound inside the chord.

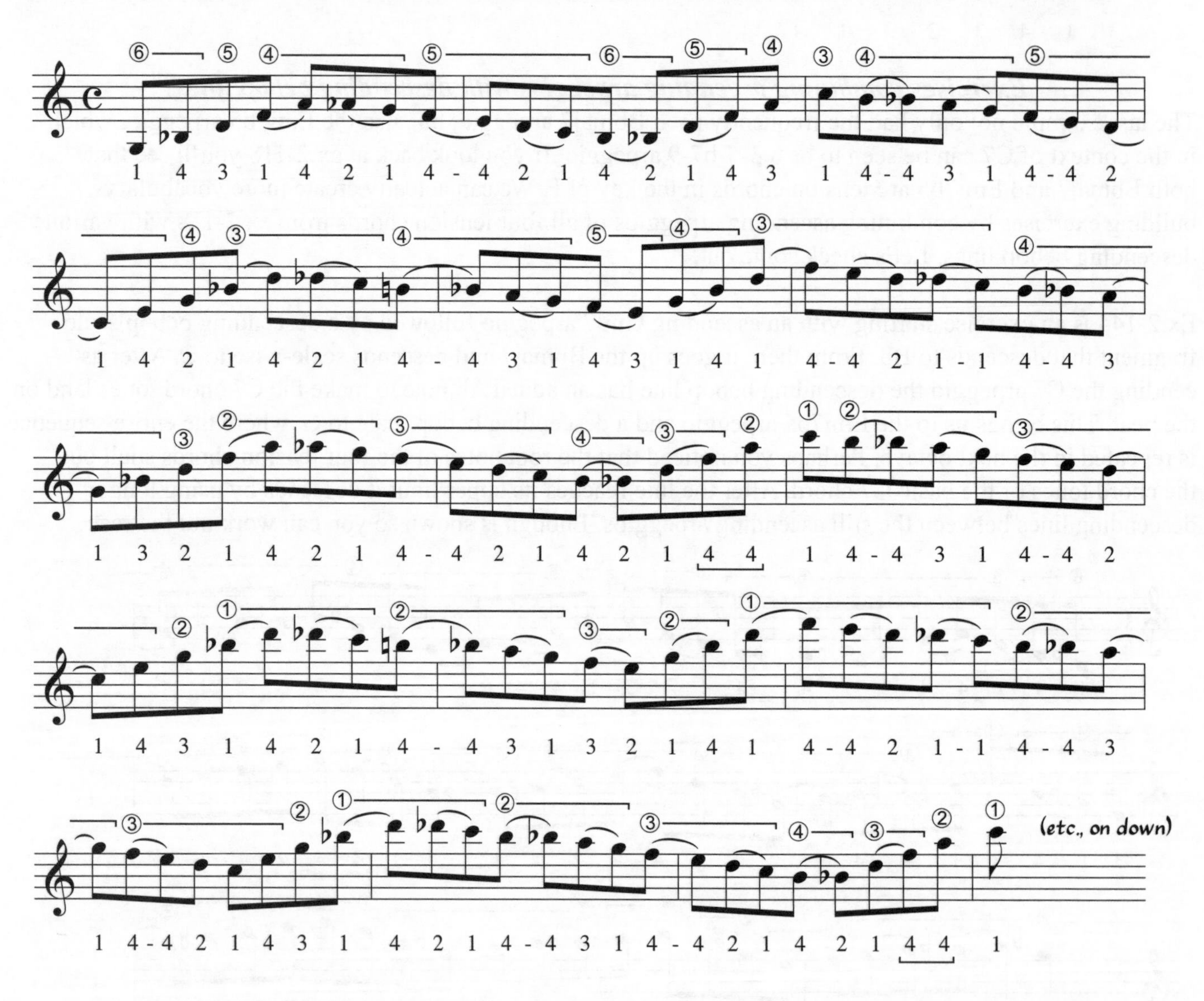

Ex.2-146 (on the following page) is the most complex exercise yet. The 7th of each arpeggio is approached from a half-step below, placing it on the beat. This becomes the first note of an approach-combination targeting the octave root of the current arpeggio, which in turn becomes the first note of an approach-combination targeting the the 7th of the current arpeggio, followed by a short descending fragment to the root of the next arpeggio, etc.

The bebop dominant scale exercises in another form on the fingerboard

Ex.2-147 shows another form for the C bebop dominant scale. It starts on a low Bb on the sixth string and, as before, uses strings and fingerings duplicated in each octave ascending and slightly modified strings and fingerings duplicated in each octave descending.

Ex.2-148 is basically 2-135 translated into the new form.

Ex.2-149 is 2-136 translated into the new form.

Ex.2-150 shows 2-137 translated into the new form.

Ex.2-151 is 2-138 translated into the new form.

Ex.2-152 is 2-139 translated into the new form.

Ex.2-153 shows 2-140 translated into the new form.

Ex.2-154 shows 2-141 translated into the new form.

Ex.2-155 is 2-142 in the new form.

Ex.2-156 shows 2-143 in the new form.

Ex.2-157 is based on 2-144, but since Bb is the lowest note in the new form it starts with an ascending Bbmaj7 arpeggio instead of Gmi7, and also ascends all the way to a high Bbmaj7 arpeggio before descending.

Ex.2-158 is based on 2-145 translated into the new form in the new range.

(continued on following page)

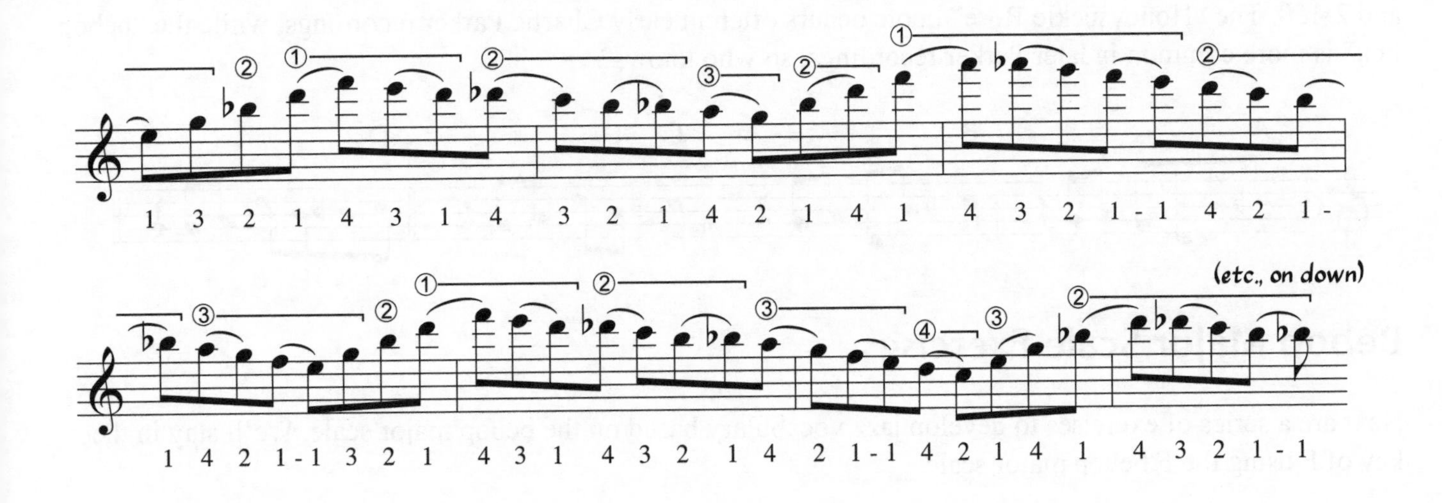

Ex.2-159 is based on 2-146 translated into the new form in the new range.

The hypothetical evolution of the "bebop lick"

Ex.2-160 shows a hypothetical evolution of what Jerry Coker and many others refer to as the "bebop lick." Each measure can be looked at separately. Measure A is the famous "Honeysuckle Rose" quote from chapter 1 (ex.1-41 transposed). Measure B is an edited version with a slight rhythmic displacement. Measure C uses an octave displacement, moving the D from measure B up an octave. Measure D adds the classic bebop dominant passing tone, the B natural between C and Bb, giving us the six-note phrase that occurs in 2-137 and 2-150. The “Honeysuckle Rose” quote occurs often in early Charlie Parker recordings, while the “bebop lick” is more common in later Parker recordings, so who knows?

Bebop Major Scale Exercises

Next are a series of exercises to develop jazz vocabulary based on the bebop major scale. We’ll stay in the key of F using the F bebop major scale.

Ex.2-161 shows an F bebop major scale. It starts on a low F on the sixth string and, as before, uses strings and fingerings duplicated in each octave ascending and slightly modified strings and fingerings duplicated in each octave descending.

Exercises using the bebop major scale to develop vocabulary for improvisation

Ex.2-162 shows a F bebop major scale in combination with a Fmaj9 arpeggio, using the arpeggio to ascend (with some chromatic passing tones added) and the scale to descend. Since it begins and ends on the same note, it can easily be converted into a practice loop.

Ex.2-163 shows a descending line featuring deflection, the old 5-to-3 device, and enclosure. Only the first octave is shown. Like the dominant exercises, the same features should be played in the next octave down, and you can use the ascending portion from 2-162 to get back to the starting note to create a practice loop.

Ex.2-164 starts with an Fmaj7 arpeggio using octave displacement to make the line descend, in combination with a chromatic enclosure of the root. The same instructions apply here that were given in 2-163.

After skipping down to the A, ex.2-165 jumps directly up to the 7th, E, and descends chromatically to the 5th before using the enclosure. Same instructions as before.

Ex.2-166 replaces the initially skipped-to A with a C# for another variation.

Ex.2-167 shows yet another variation. By now you can do the analysis for yourself.

Ex.2-168 is an ascending line using familiar material including a double-approach from both below and above the 5th, C.

Exercises combining ascending arpeggios with descending bebop major lines

This next set of exercises combines ascending arpeggios from each chord tone of F6 (Fmaj7, Ami7, C7, and Dmi7) with descending bebop lines based on the F bebop major scale.

Ex.2-169 combines the basic four-note 7th chords with the descending bebop fragments. Only the first five bars are shown. Continue in the same fashion as you did in the bebop dominant exercises, up and down the full range. In the following examples only a little more than the first octave of each exercise is shown, enough so you can work out the entire studies.

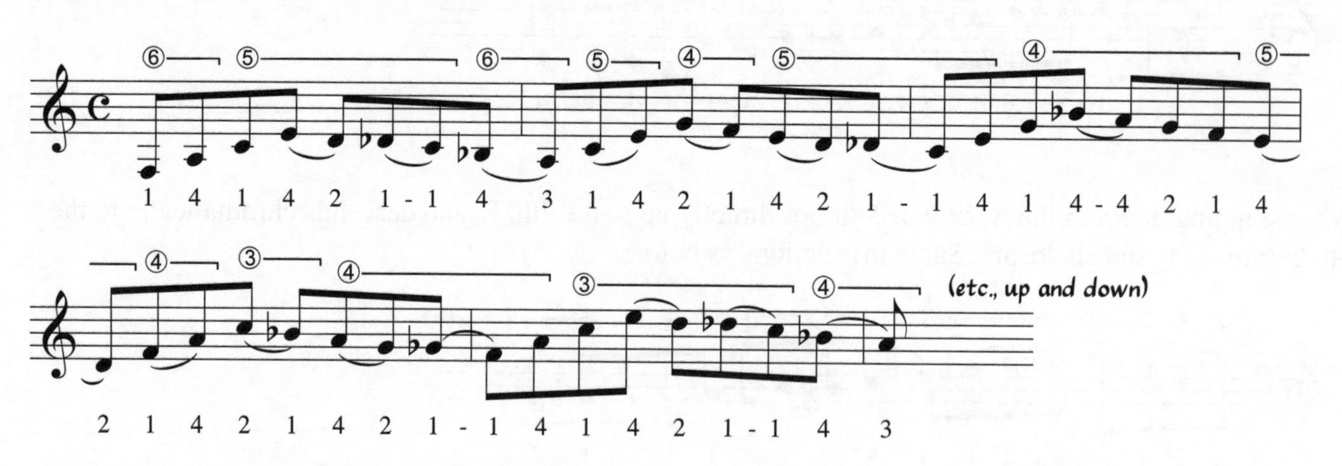

Ex.2-170 combines the ascending five-note 9th chords with the appropriate descending lines.

Ex.2-171 is based on the same scheme as used in 2-146, but in our current F bebop major scale.

(continued on next page)

The bebop major scale exercises in another form on the fingerboard

Ex.2-172 shows the F bebop major scale starting on the 3rd, A, on the sixth string and, as before, uses strings and fingerings duplicated in each octave ascending and slightly modified strings and fingerings duplicated in each octave descending.

Ex.2-173 is based on 2-162 translated into the new form. Since the register has changed, things are switched around a bit, but you can see it's based on the same idea.

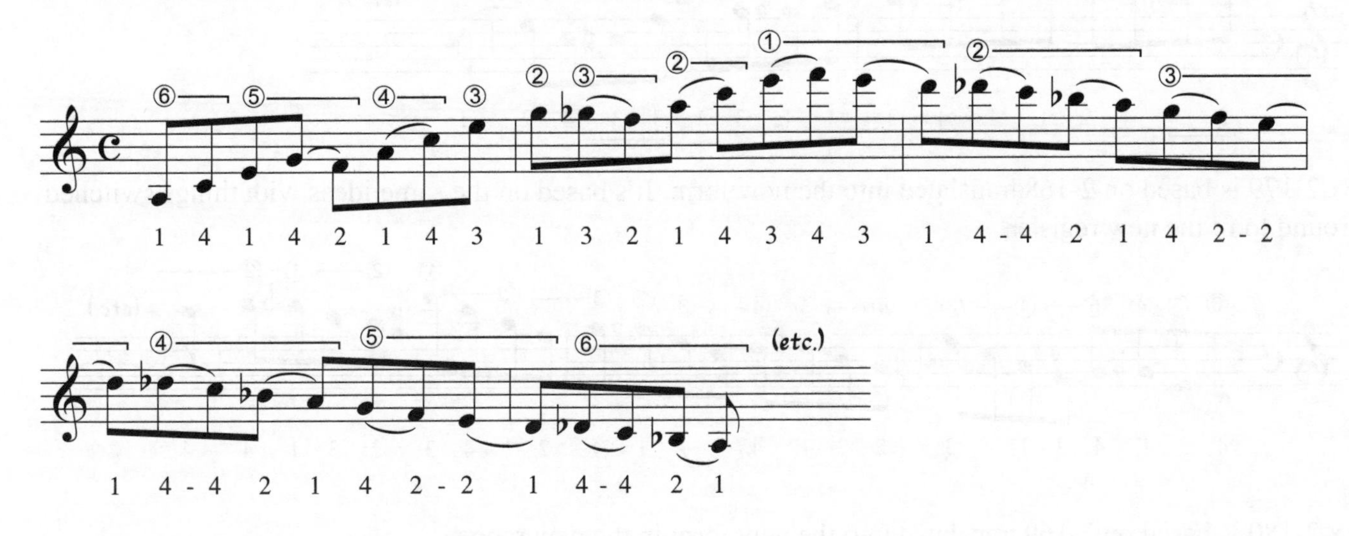

Ex.2-174 is based on 2-163 translated into the new form and raised an octave to fit the new register.

Ex.2-175 is based on 2-164 translated into the new form and raised an octave to fit the new register.

Ex.2-176 is based on 2-165 translated into the new form and raised an octave to fit the new register.

Ex.2-177 is based on 2-166 translated into the new form and raised an octave to fit the new register.

Ex.2-178 is based on 2-167 translated into the new form and raised an octave to fit the new register.

Ex.2-179 is based on 2-168 translated into the new form. It's based on the same ideas with things switched around to fit the new register.

Ex.2-180 is based on 2-169 translated into the new form in the new range.

(continued on next page)

Ex.2-181 is based on 2-170 translated into the new form in the new range.

Ex.2-182 is based on 2-171 translated into the new form in the new range.

More Forms and Keys for the Bebop Dominant and Major Scales

So far we have been practicing in bebop dominant scale forms with the 5th as the lowest note and the 7th as the lowest note, and in bebop major scale forms with the root as the lowest note and the 3rd as the lowest note. To be complete we need bebop dominant scale forms with the root and with the 3rd as the lowest notes, and bebop major scale forms with the 5th and with the 6th as the lowest notes. To do this let's change keys to make the forms more user-friendly (and easier to read), and to start playing the ideas in different keys.

Bebop dominant scale forms with the root and with the 3rd as the lowest notes

Ex.2-183 shows a form for the F bebop dominant scale with the root as the lowest note. It uses strings and fingerings duplicated in each octave ascending and slightly modified strings and fingerings duplicated in each octave descending, as usual. Your homework assignment is to work out exercises that correspond to all the bebop dominant scale exercises we've done so far, but transposed into the new key and form. You can write them out if absolutely necessary, but it would be better if you can do it without notation. After all, this is training for improvising by ear, not for reading practice.

Ex.2-184 shows a form for the Eb bebop dominant scale with the 3rd as the lowest note. The homework assignment is the same as in 2-183.

Bebop major scale forms with the 5th and with the 6th as the lowest notes

Ex.2-185 shows a form for the C bebop major scale with the 5th as the lowest note. Your homework assignment is to work out exercises that correspond to all the bebop major scale exercises we've done so far, but transposed into the new key and form.

Ex.2-186 shows a form for the Bb bebop major scale with the 6th as the lowest note. The homework assignment is the same as in 2-185.

Exercises on the Bebop Melodic Minor Scale

Up until now we've been focusing on the bebop dominant scale and the bebop major scale, the two that are emphasized by David Baker, who may have actually originated the term "bebop scale." There are many possible bebop scales that I'm not going to cover here. If you're curious (and I hope you are), check out *Forward Motion* by Hal Galper and *Jazz Line* by Jerry Bergonzi. There are a couple of bebop minor scales that I'd like to mention, however. One is the bebop natural minor scale, which is identical to its relative major bebop scale. All of the F bebop major scale exercises, for example, are also D bebop natural minor scale exercises. The other minor that is important in this context is called the bebop melodic minor scale. It is the same as its parallel major bebop scale but with a minor 3rd, so we can create F bebop melodic minor scales by flatting the A notes in our F bebop major scales.

Ex.2-187 shows the strings and fingerings for F bebop melodic minor with F as the lowest note. When you do your homework and convert all the major exercises to melodic minor, you should be aware that the minor 3rd changes how certain situations get handled, so I'll show you some to demonstrate.

Ex.2-188 is based on 2-163 converted to melodic minor. The 5-to-3 device has been modified to target the minor 3rd.

Ex.2-189 is based on the fourth bar of 2-169. Since there is a whole-step between the Bb and the Ab, the half-step is used right away between those notes.

Ex.2-190 is extracted from the second and third measures of 2-170 converted to minor. Again the passing note has been moved to place the second Ab on the beat.

In ex.2-191, based on the third and fourth bars of 2-171, the last two notes of the first bar are modified to target the Ab.

The F bebop melodic minor scale in another form on the fingerboard

Ex.2-192 shows the F bebop melodic minor scale in another form on the fingerboard along with the new fingering. It has the minor 3rd, Ab, as the lowest note. I'm through writing out every example, so you'll have to convert all the major exercises into this new minor form.

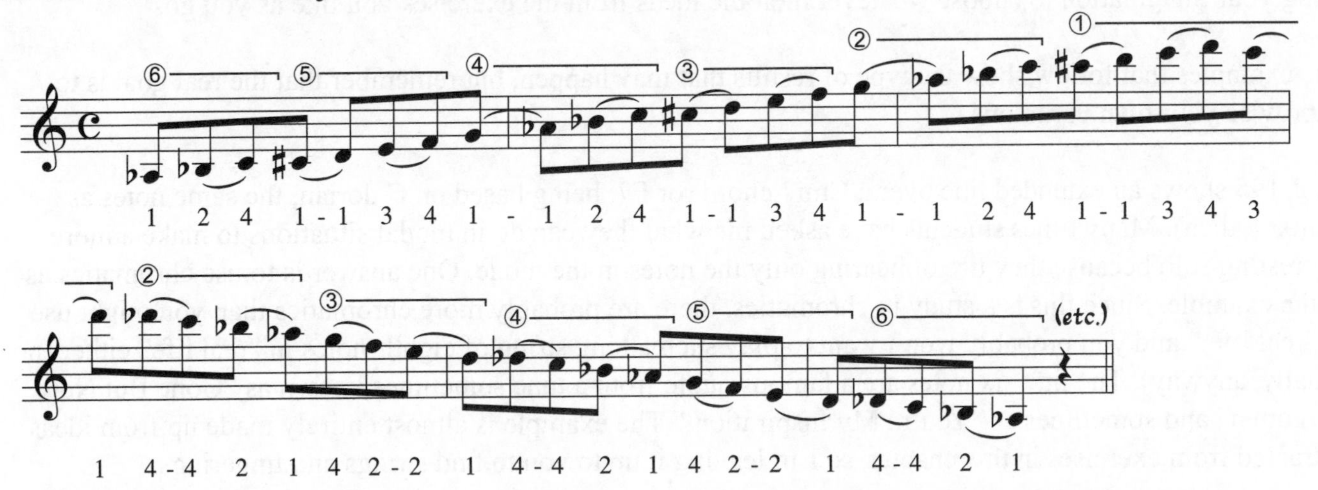

The C bebop melodic minor scale with the 5th as the lowest note

Ex.2-193 shows the strings and fingerings for the C bebop melodic minor scale with the 5th, G, as the lowest note. You know what your assignment is.

The Bb bebop melodic minor scale with the 6th as the lowest note

Ex.2-194 shows the strings and fingerings for the Bb bebop melodic minor scale with the 6th, G, as the lowest note. Same homework assignment.

"Inside" Chromatic Wrap-Up

One way to practice using all of these chromatic ideas is to improvise long extended lines over one chord, using your imagination to choose whatever melodic ideas from the exercises you like as you go.

The examples that follow show the type of results that may happen, but remember that the real goal is to improvise your own variations.

Ex.2-195 shows an extended line over a Cmi7 chord (or F7, being based on C dorian, the same notes as F mixolydian). Many times students have asked me what they can do in modal situations to make a more interesting solo because they tire of hearing only the notes in the mode. One answer is to use chromatics as in the example. Since this is a study in chromatics, there are probably more chromatics than you might use in "real life," and you probably won't want to play such a long string of eighth-notes in "real life" either (not usually, anyway). The first six notes are a famous quote from a tune sometimes known as "Gone But Not Forgotten" and sometimes as "You're My Inspiration." The example is almost entirely made up from ideas extracted from exercises in this chapter, so I'm leaving it up to you to find strings and fingerings.

Ex.2-196 shows an extended line over a Cmaj7 chord.

Ex.2-197 shows an extended line over a Cmi-maj7 chord. It is based on 2-196 converted into melodic minor.

Just one final example before we move on. Ex.2-198 shows a line for Cmi7 and/or F7. It starts with the first five notes of the "Gone But Not Forgotten-You're My Inspiration" quote and continues with the old 5-to3 device (in relation to F7). Then from the A note at the beginning of the second measure the line is entirely derived from two major triads, F and Eb, a mutually-exclusive (no common tones) triad-pair that forms a hexatonic pitch-collection that can be used to create interesting melodies for modal type situations with a different, more "open" style than the previous chromatic lines. Let's check out some of these hexatonic triad-pairs next.

Chapter 3 – Hexatonics Revisited: Mutually-Exclusive Triad-Pairs

Play ex.3-1, the first twelve bars of a famous solo recorded by McCoy Tyner on piano over F7sus4, or more accurately, F mixolydian. Every note in the example belongs to either an F major triad or an Eb major triad.

After venturing "outside" for a few bars, ex.3-2 shows a return by McCoy to the same two triads as before.

These examples demonstrate how much of the "modal" and "fourthy" sounds of this idiom are actually derived from these triad-pairs. McCoy's left hand voicings behind these lines are primarily three-note fourth chords that are diatonic to the F mixolydian mode.

Definition of triad-pair

A triad pair could be any two triads, but what we mean when we use the term here is two triads that have no notes in common, resulting in a six-note, or hexatonic, collection. A more accurate name would be "mutually-exclusive triad-pair", but that's too long so we'll just use "triad-pair" for short. Triad-pairs that have both triads belonging to the same seven-note scale are always adjacent triads, that is, their roots are next to each other in the scale, such as I and II or IV and V. Major and minor triad-pairs a tritone apart can be found in the eight-note diminished scale.

Most of the popular triad-pairs use two major triads or two minor triads, but mixed versions and versions using diminished and augmented triads also exist and are used. For a complete study of all the types of triad-pairs check out *Triad Pairs For Jazz* by Gary Campbell (Alfred Publishing Co.), *Hexatonics* by Jerry Bergonzi (Advanced Music), and *Intervalic Improvisation* by Walt Weiskopf (Jamey Aebersold Jazz). This book will focus mostly on two major triads a whole-step apart, but we'll also touch on some other useful combinations as well.

Two major triads a whole-step apart, hereafter called the major whole-step pair, can be found in the major scale and all of its modes, and also in the melodic minor scale and all of its modes as well, making it extremely useful. To gain some improvisational fluency with the major whole-step pair let's use the Eb-F pair that McCoy used in the examples above and develop some positional fingerings and exercises to start.

Positional fingerings for the major whole-step pair

Keep in mind that this Eb-F major whole-step triad-pair can be used for F mixolydian (F7sus), C dorian (Cmi7), Eb lydian (Ebmaj7#11), Eb lydian dominant (Eb7#11), G locrian #2 (Gmi9b5), and A7alt among many others.

The Eb-F major whole-step pair fingerings and exercises in the third and second positions

Ex.3-3A shows an across-the-board fingering for an Eb major triad arpeggio in the third position, while 3-3B shows an across-the-board fingering for an F major triad arpeggio in the third and second positions. These forms show us where our first triad-pair studies will take place.

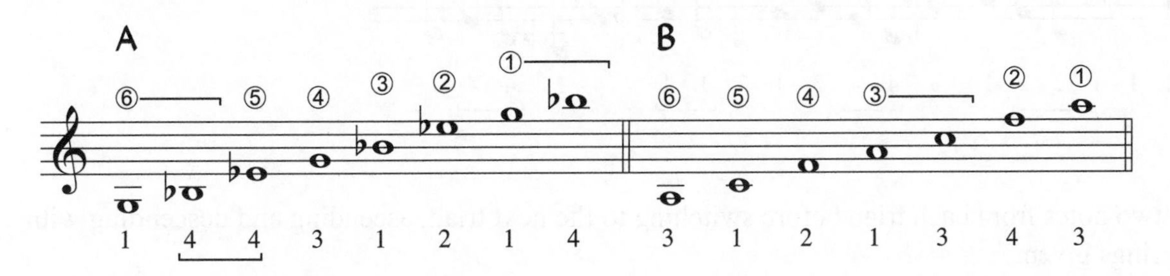

Ex.3-4 shows the major whole-step pair going up the three-note triad inversions as arpeggios ascending and descending in linear order in the third and second positions with strings and fingerings given.

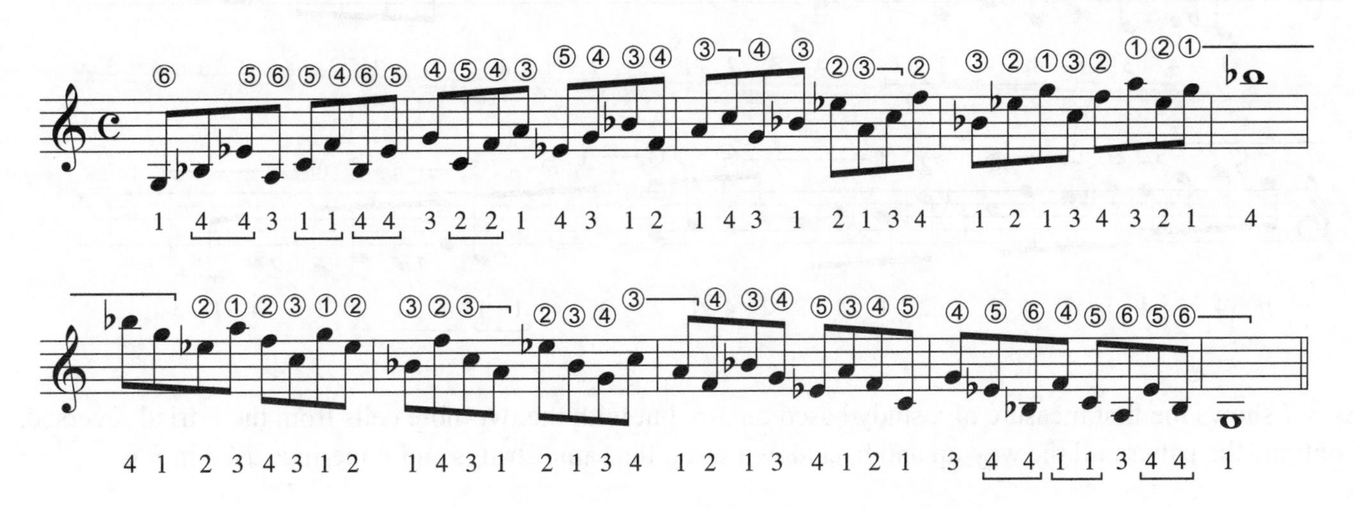

Ex.3-5 shows the same three-note triad inversions converted into four-note cells begining and ending on the top note of each with strings and fingerings given.

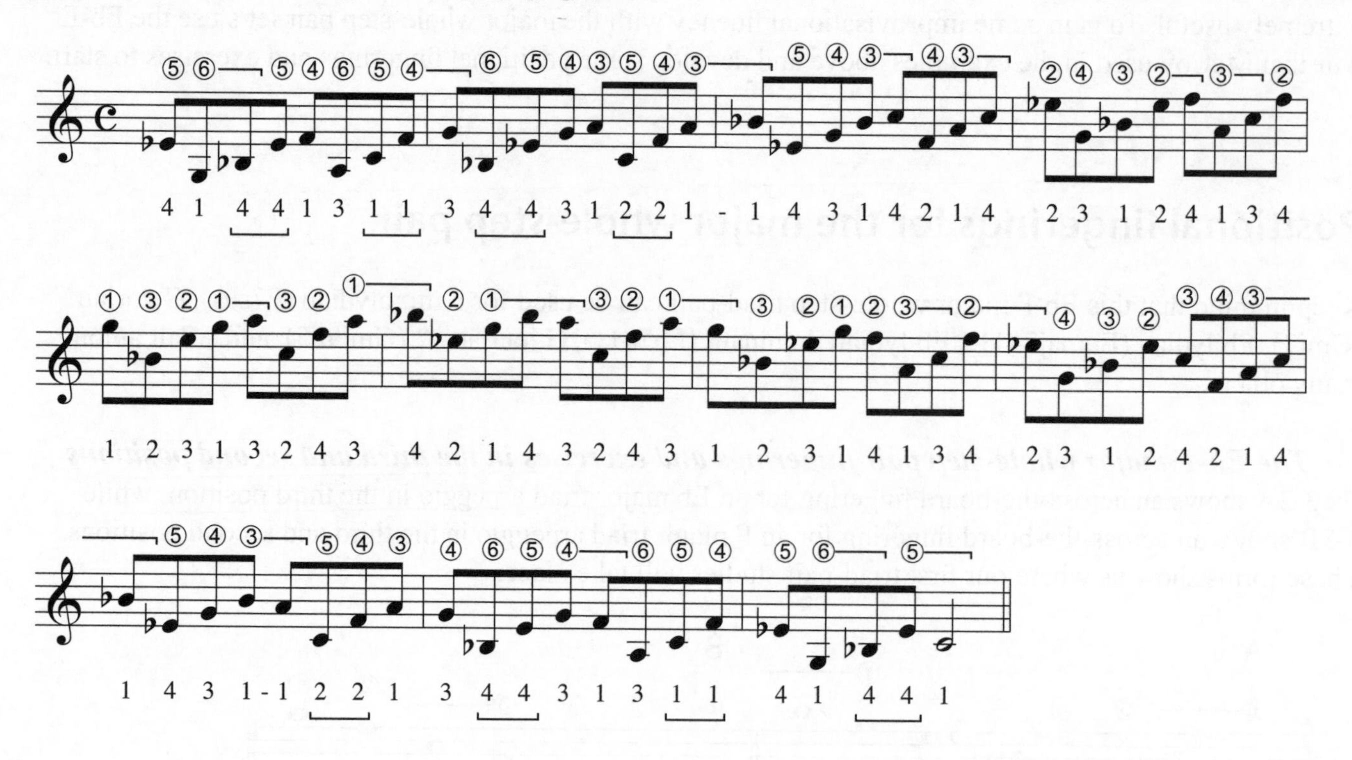

Ex.3-6 has only two notes from each triad before switching to the next triad, ascending and descending with strings and fingerings given.

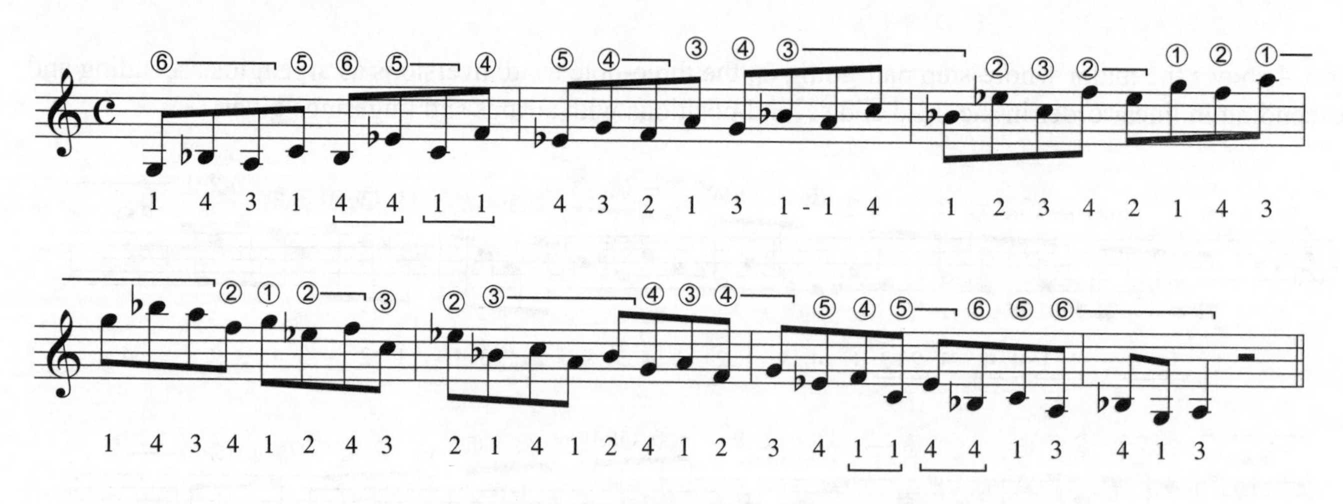

Ex.3-7 shows the first measure of a study based on 3-6, but with the two-note cells from the F triad reversed. Continue the pattern all the way up and back down using the same strings and fingerings used in 3-6.

Ex.3-8 shows the first measure of another study based on 3-6, but with the two-note cells from the Eb triad reversed this time. Continue the pattern all the way up and back down using the same strings and fingerings used in 3-6.

Ex.3-9 is also based on two-notes per triad, but skipping in sixths and fifths. It is shown ascending and descending with strings and fingerings given.

Ex.3-10 is the major whole-step pair going up the three-note triad inversions as arpeggios ascending and descending in linear order again, but in open-voiced triads this time, creating a wider more angular sound. It is shown ascending and descending with strings and fingerings given.

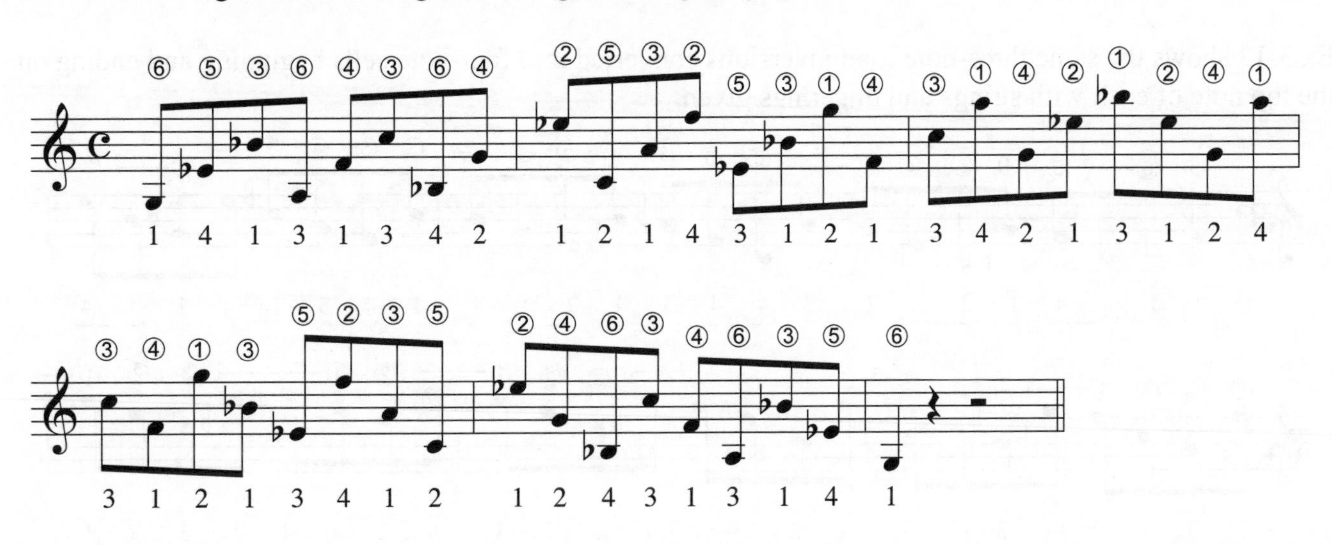

The Eb-F major whole-step pair fingerings and exercises in the fifth and sixth positions

On the following page, ex.3-11A shows an across-the-board fingering for an F major triad arpeggio in the fifth position, while 3-11B shows an across-the-board fingering for an Eb major triad arpeggio in the fifth and sixth positions.

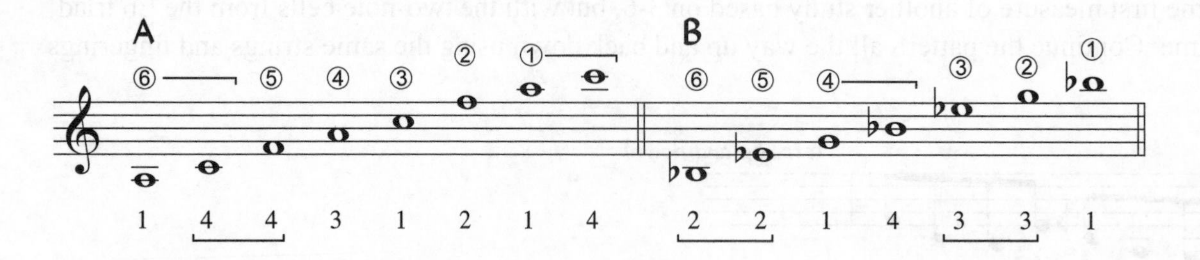

Ex.3-12 shows the major whole-step pair going up the three-note triad inversions as arpeggios ascending and descending in linear order in the fifth and sixth positions with strings and fingerings given.

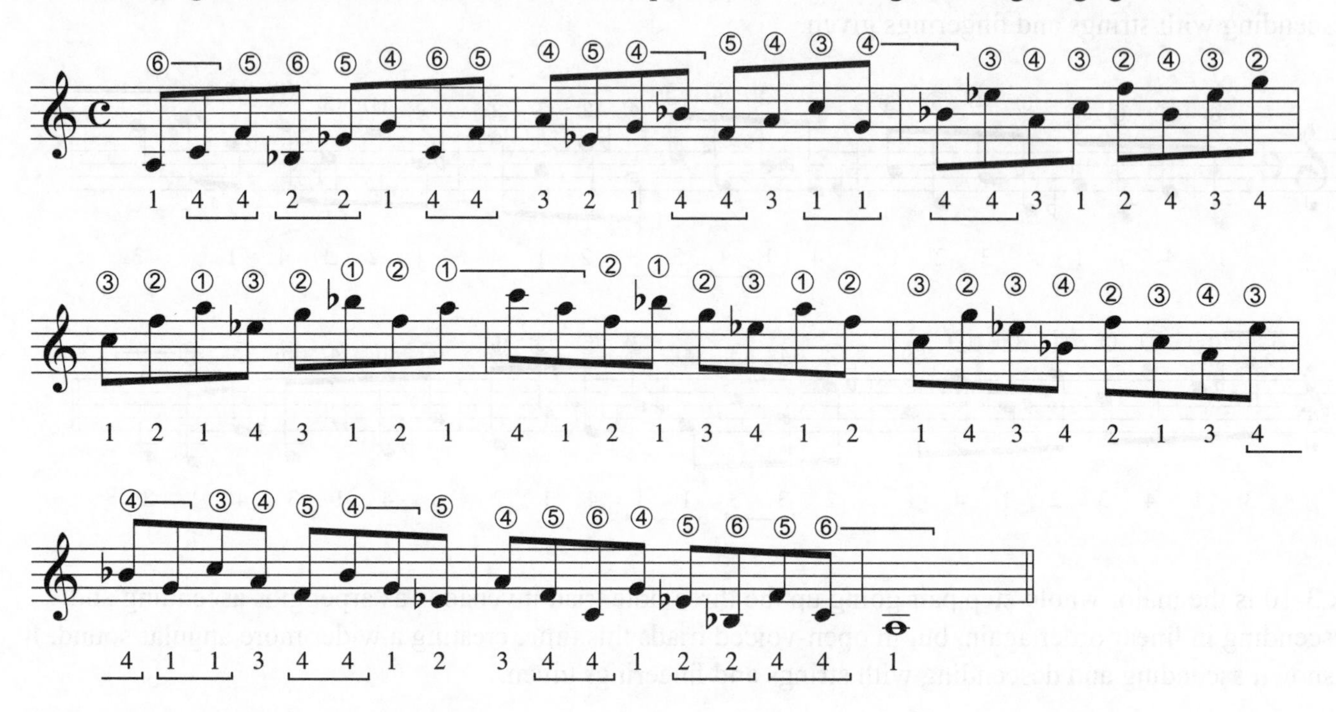

Ex.3-13 shows the same three-note triad inversions converted into four-note cells beginning and ending on the top note of each with strings and fingerings given.

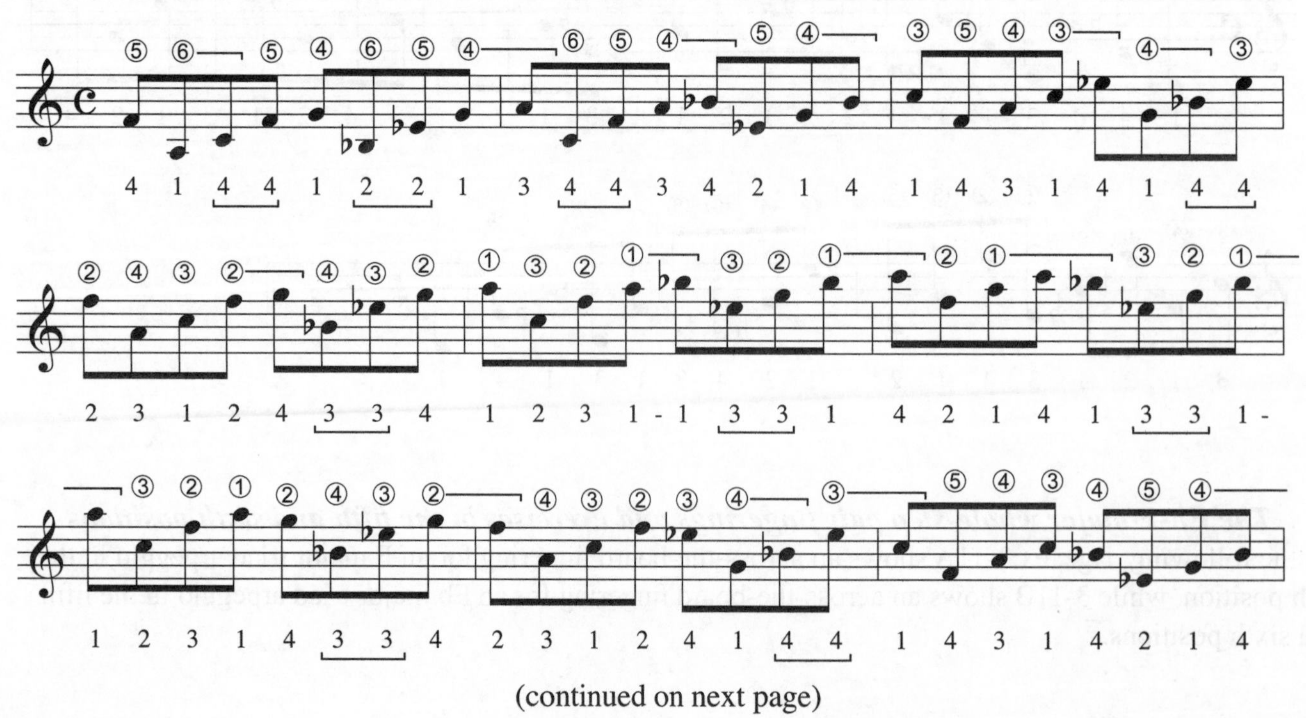

(continued on next page)

Ex.3-14 is the pattern from 3-6 moved into the fifth and sixth positions. The first eight notes of the ascending and descending forms are shown. You can easily work out fingerings from the arpeggios in 3-11.

Ex.3-15 reverses the the two-note Eb triad cells. Only the first bar is shown so complete the pattern up and back down.

Ex.3-16 reverses the the two-note F triad cells. Same instructions as in ex.3-15.

Now your assignment is to work out exercises in the fifth and sixth positions based on the patterns from 3-9 and 3-10.

The Eb-F major whole-step pair fingerings and exercises in the seventh and eighth positions

Ex.3-17A shows an across-the-board fingering for an F major triad arpeggio in the seventh and eighth positions, while 3-17B shows an across-the-board fingering for an Eb major triad arpeggio in the eighth position.

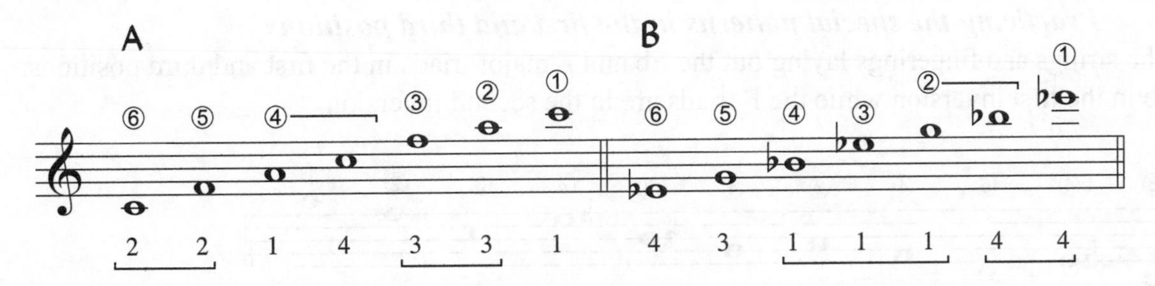

Using all the above whole-step pair studies as models, work out all the complete exercises for the Eb-F pair in the seventh and eighth positions.

The Eb-F major whole-step pair fingerings and exercises in the tenth position

Ex.3-18A shows an across-the-board fingering for an Eb major triad arpeggio in the tenth position, while 3-18B shows an across-the-board fingering for an F major triad arpeggio in the tenth position.

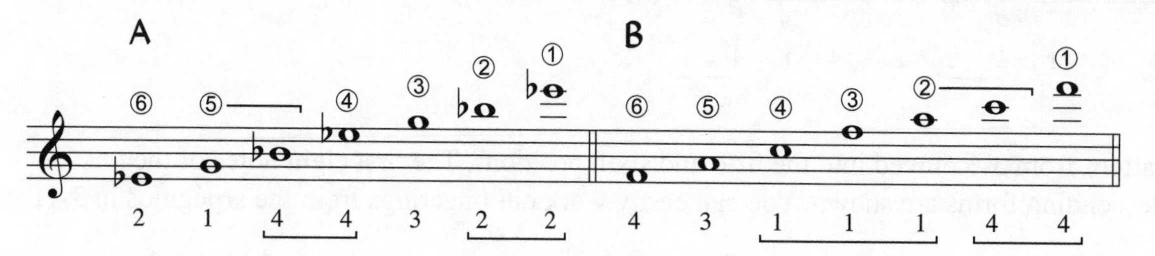

Using all the above whole-step pair studies as models, work out all the complete exercises for the Eb-F pair in the tenth position.

The Eb-F major whole-step pair fingerings and exercises in the twelfth and thirteenth positions

Ex.3-19A shows an across-the-board fingering for an F major triad arpeggio in the twelfth position, while 3-19B shows an across-the-board fingering for an Eb major triad arpeggio in the twelfth and thirteenth positions.

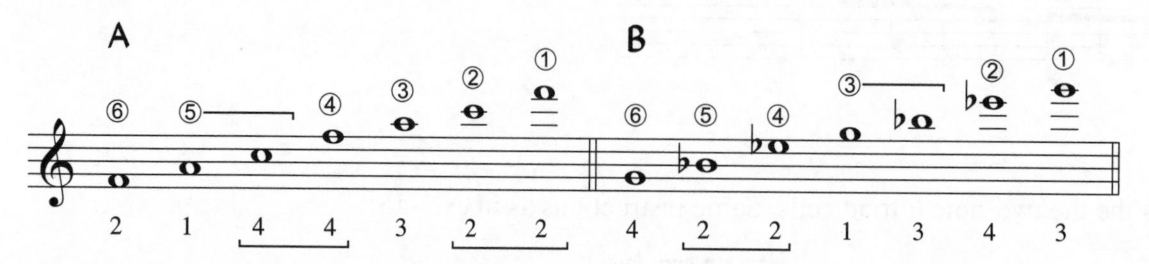

Using all the above whole-step pair studies as models, work out all the complete exercises for the Eb-F pair in the twelfth and thirteenth positions.

Special Patterns Combining Adjacent Positions

Some melodic patterns derived from triad-pairs lie nicely on the guitar when the triads are spread across three strings each, with the same inversions occuring in two different octaves. This produces fingerboard patterns that combine two adjacent postions. In this case "adjacent" means two to four frets away so the same inversions spread across the strings the same way in both octaves.

Practicing the special patterns in the first and third positions

Ex.3-20 shows the strings and fingerings laying out the Eb and F major triads in the first and third positions. The Eb triads are in the first inversion while the F triads are in the second inversion.

⑥ ⑤ ④ ⑤ ④ ③ ④ ③ ② ③ ② ①

3 1 1 3 3 2 3 1 2 3 4 3

Ex.3-21 shows the first pattern. It goes straight up the triad inversions in order, and reverses back down. Since the first triad is Eb, the pickup note is from the F triad, and since the last triad (ascending) is F, the resolution note is from the Eb triad. The same concept is applied descending.

Ex.3-22 returns to the middle note of each triad inversion, creating four-note cells. Some fingerings are slightly modified to make the pattern more practical.

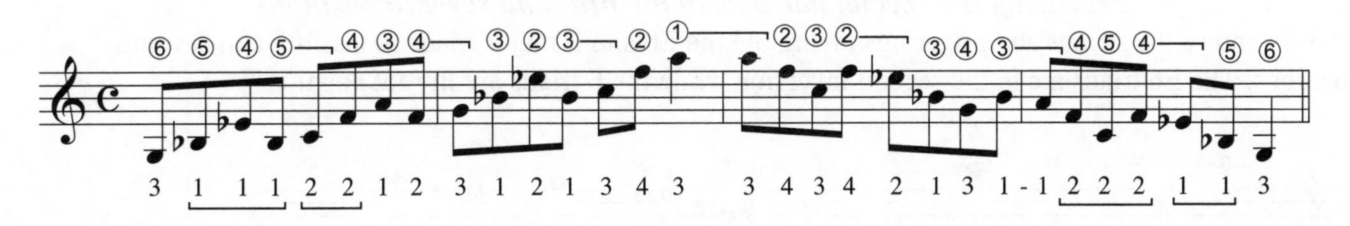

Ex.3-23 first uses three notes from the Eb triad and one from the F triad to form a four-note cell, followed by a four-note cell using two notes from each triad, and finally one note from Eb and three from F before duplicating the pattern in the next octave. The pickup and resolution notes follow the same concept used in 3-21.

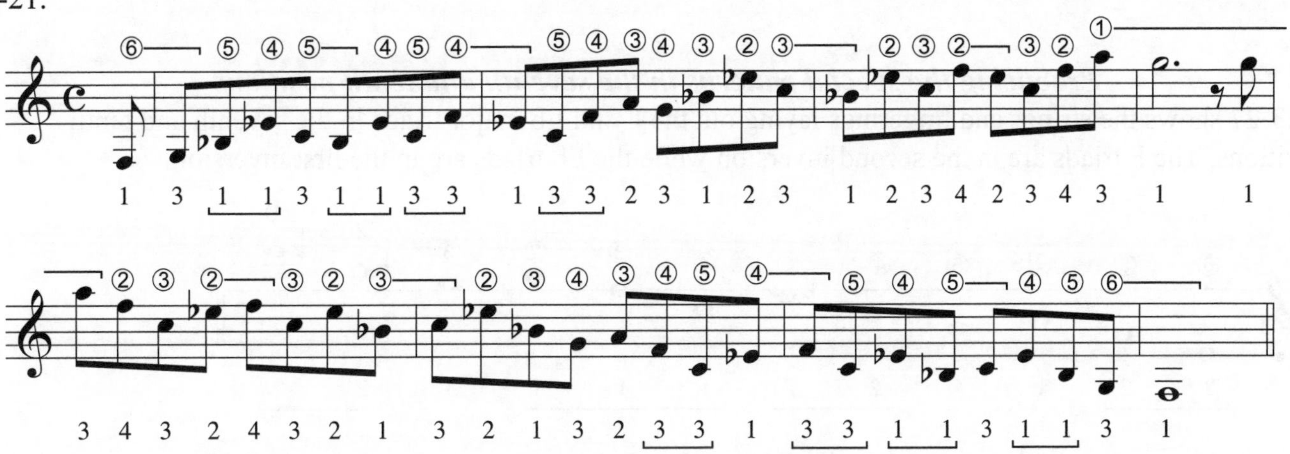

Practicing the special patterns in the third and fifth positions

Ex.3-24 shows the strings and fingerings laying out the F and Eb major triads in the third and fifth positions. The F triads are in the first inversion while the Eb triads are in root position.

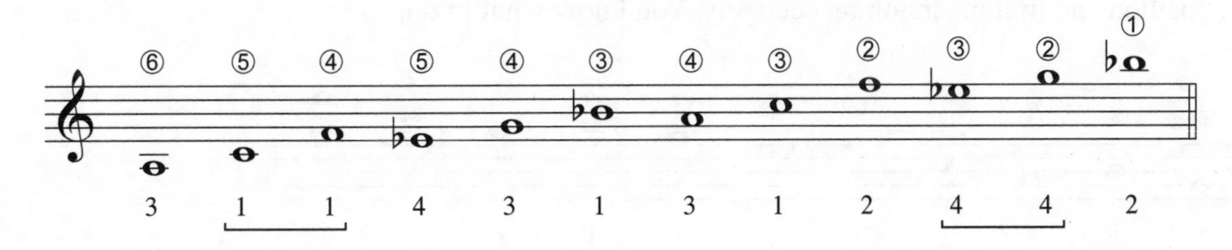

Creating exercises based on 3-21 and 3-22 in the fingerings and locations shown in 3-24 should be relatively simple, but transfering the melodic pattern from 3-23 could be tricky, so ex.3-25 shows the notes. You can work out the fingerings.

Practicing the special patterns in the fifth and seventh positions

Ex.3-26 shows the strings and fingerings laying out the Eb and F major triads in the fifth and seventh positions. The Eb triads are in the second inversion while the F triads are in root position.

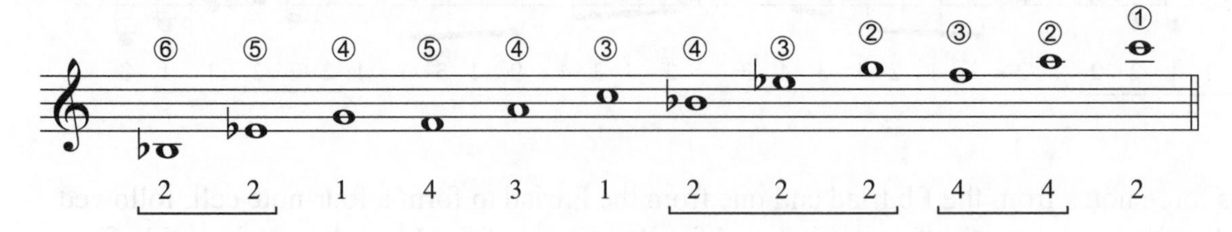

Your homework assignment is to work out all of the studies in the new positions shown in 3-26.

Practicing the special patterns in the seventh and tenth positions

Ex.3-27 shows the strings and fingerings laying out the F and Eb major triads in the seventh and tenth positions. The F triads are in the second inversion while the Eb triads are in the first inversion.

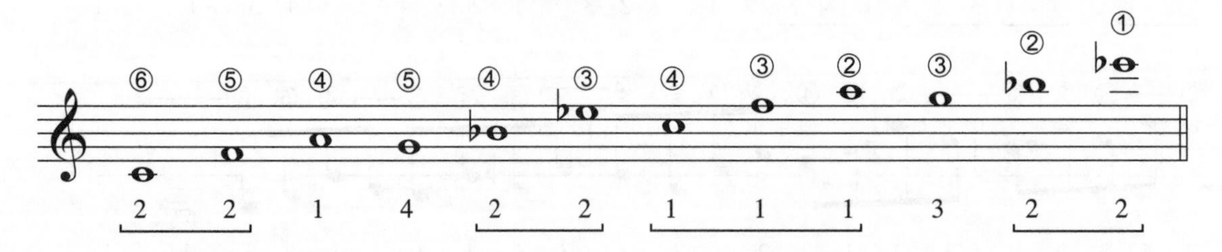

Again, your assignment is to work out all of the studies in the new positions shown in 3-27.

Practicing the special patterns in the eighth through twelfth positions

Ex.3-28 shows the strings and fingerings laying out the Eb and F major triads in the eighth through twelfth positions, in root position and first inversion respectively. You know what to do.

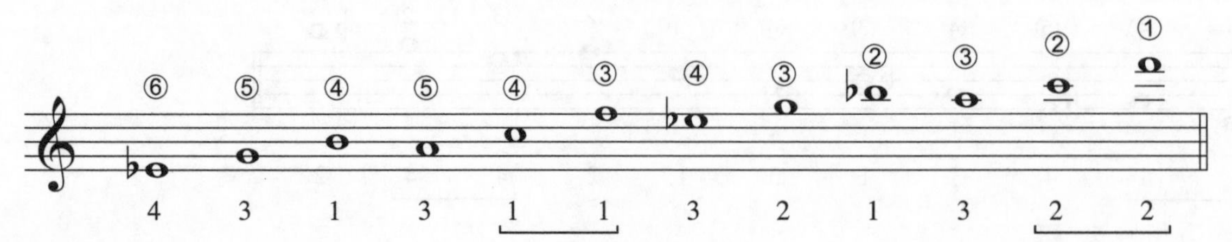

Practicing the special patterns in the tenth through thirteenth positions

Ex.3-29 shows the strings and fingerings laying out the F and Eb major triads in the tenth through thirteenth positions, in root position and second inversion respectively. Work out all of the exercises.

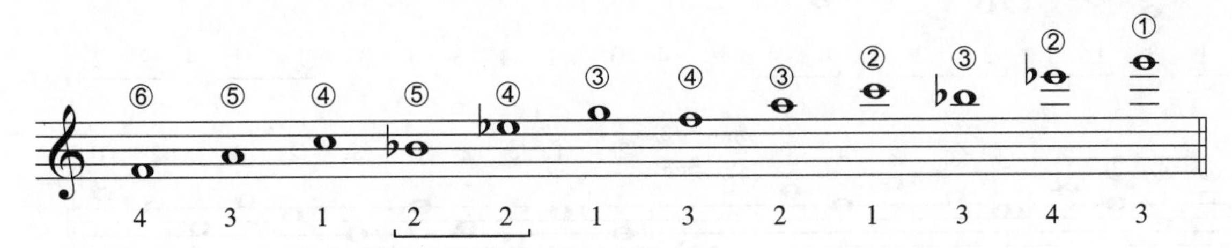

Long Fingerboard Patterns for the Major Whole-Step Pair

Now let's look at some long fingerboard patterns. First we'll try some patterns that move up the fingerboard along a constant set of strings. Then we'll check out some full-range patterns that go up and across the fingerboard.

Long patterns going up a constant set of strings

Ex.3-30 shows the F-Eb major whole-step pair going up the fingerboard along the fourth, third, and second strings. Use this pattern to play the melodic exercises demonstrated in examples 3-4 through 3-9.

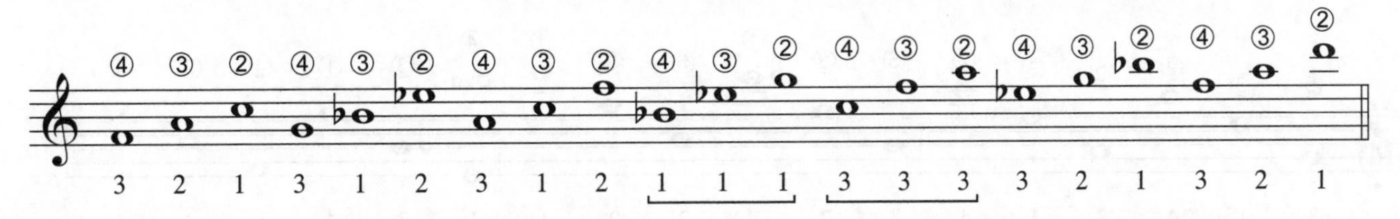

Work out this closed-position triad-pair along other sets of three consecutive strings as well.

Ex.3-31 shows the open-voiced Eb-F triad-pair going up the fingerboard along the fourth, third, and first strings. Use this pattern to play the melodic exercises demonstrated in examples 3-9 and 3-10.

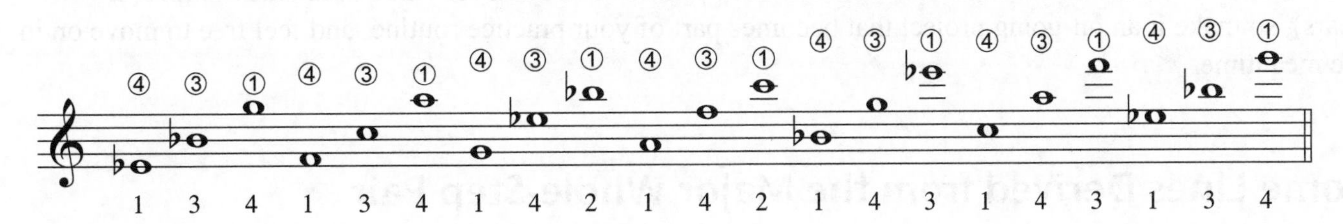

Experiment with other string and finger combinations.

Full-range patterns going up and across the fingerboard

Ex.3-32 (on the following page) shows the closed-position Eb-F major triad-pair going up and across the fingerboard, covering the full-range. I've spread each triad across three strings, but many are practical when reduced to two strings, so please experiment with alternate choices. Use this pattern to play the melodic exercises demonstrated in examples 3-4 through 3-9.

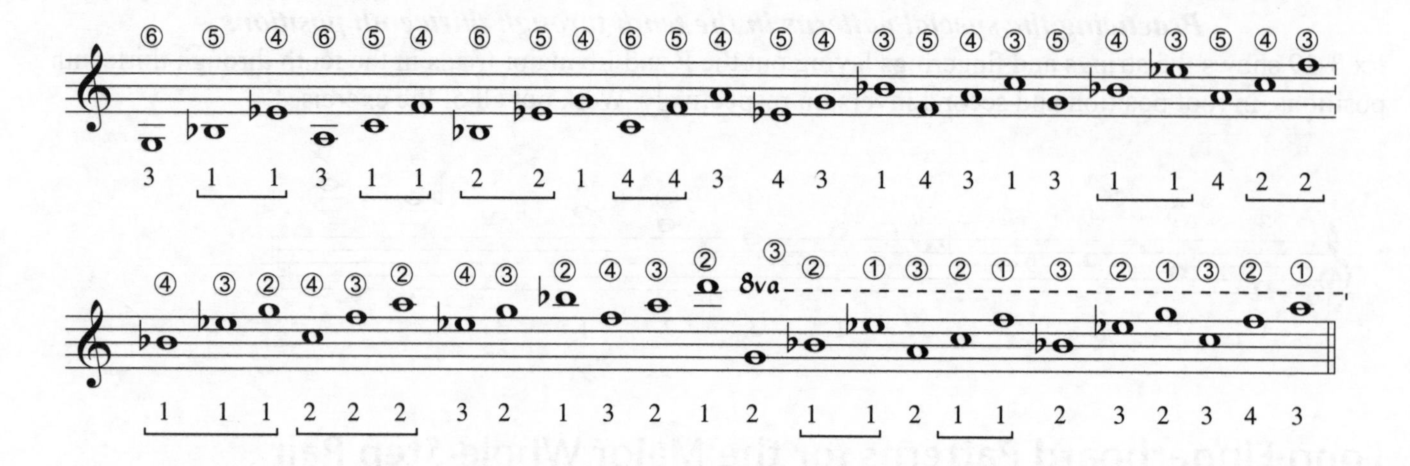

Ex.3-33 shows the open-voiced Eb-F triad-pair going up and across the fingerboard, covering the full-range. Use this pattern to play the melodic exercises demonstrated in examples 3-9 and 3-10.

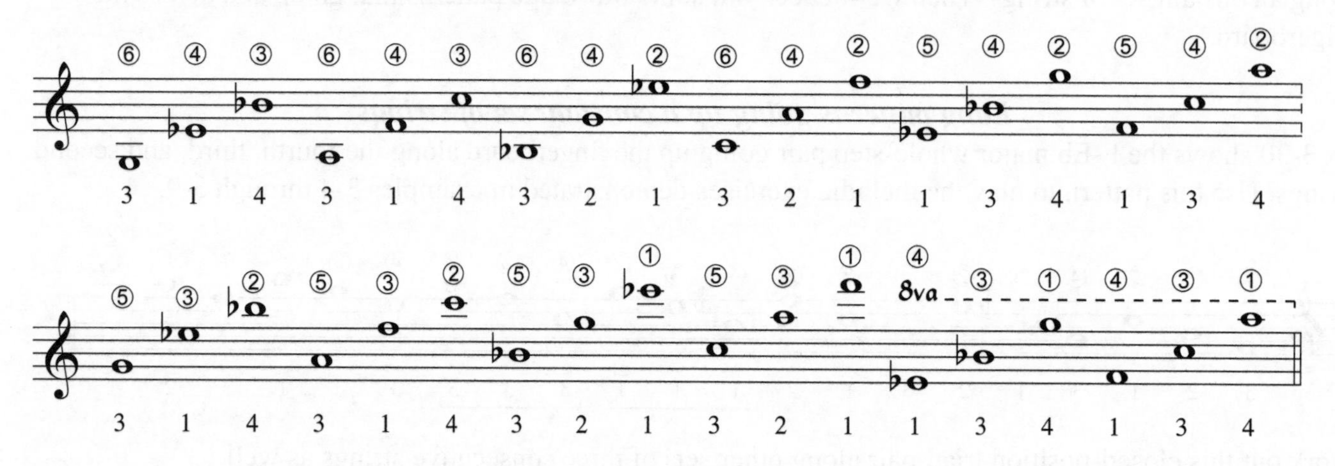

I've only shown one possible string-finger combination, so as usual experiment with other string and finger combinations.

Of course all these studies should be worked out and practiced in all keys. This could take months (or years), so make it an on-going project that becomes part of your practice routine, and feel free to move on in the meantime.

Some Lines Derived from the Major Whole-Step Pair

Now let's play a few sample lines derived from the Eb-F major whole-step triad-pair.

Ex.3-34

(continued on next page)

Ex.3-35

Ex.3-36

Ex.3-37

Notice that there are no chord symbols. The major whole-step pair is very flexible and can be used over many different chords. All of the Eb-F pair examples can be played over F7, F7sus, Cmi7, Ebmaj7#11, Eb7#11, and A7alt, to name a few. Since there is a major whole-step pair for mi7 chords, a major whole-step pair for alt Dominant chords, and a major whole-step pair for maj7#11 chords, we can create some interesting lines for II-V-I progressions.

Using major whole-step triad-pairs on II-V-I progressions

Let's try II-V-I in C major. The II chord, Dmi7, is compatible with the dorian mode, so the major whole-step triad-pair would be F and G. The V chord, G7alt, is compatible with Ab melodic minor, so the major whole-step triad-pair would be Db and Eb. The I chord, in this case Cmaj7#11, is compatible with the lydian mode, so the major whole-step triad-pair would be C and D. Examples 3-38 through 3-41 demonstrate.

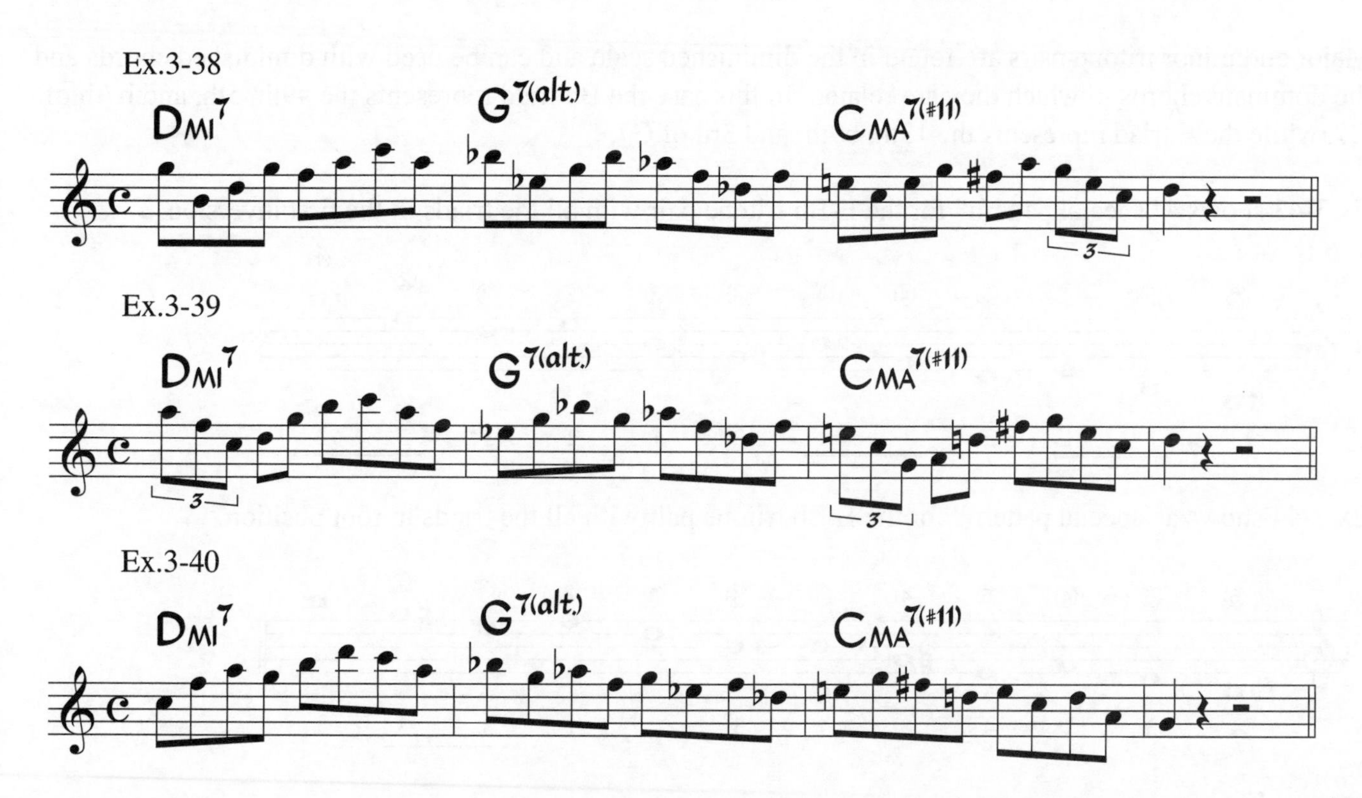

Ex.3-41

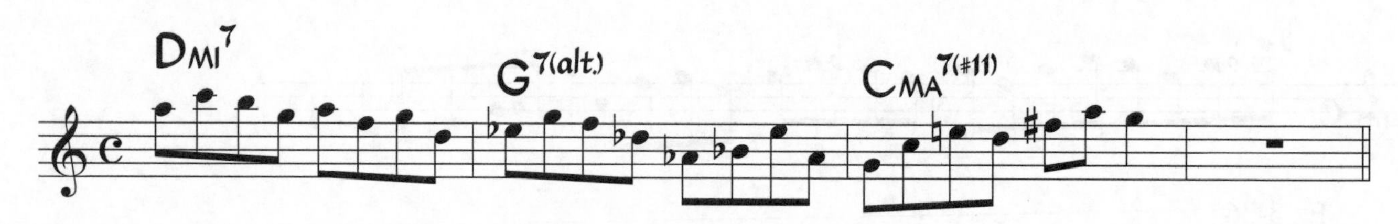

All these lines are just samples used to demonstrate the concepts. Use them as models to start creating your own lines. As you get the hang of it, you'll be able to start improvising with whole-step pairs.

A Brief Look at Some Other Triad Pairs

As mentioned earlier, this chapter focuses mainly on the major whole-step pair, but I'd like to touch on a few others, such as the major tritone pair, the minor-major whole-step pair, and the minor half-step pair. Many others are possible. For more complete coverage please refer to the works mentioned above by Campbell, Bergonzi, and Weiskopf. You can use all the fingerings, positions, and exercises from this chapter as models to work out their studies on the guitar.

The major tritone pair

Play ex.3-42. It's a II-V-I line in C major that is very similar to the last four examples. The II chord and the I chord both use the same major whole-step pairs as before, but the V chord uses a major tritone pair (two major triads a tritone apart), a Bb triad and an E triad.

Major and minor tritone pairs are found in the diminished scale and can be used with diminished chords and the dominant chords to which they are related. In this case the Bb triad represents the #9th, 5th, and b7th of G7, while the E triad represents the 13th, b9th, and 3rd of G7.

Ex.3-43 shows a "special pattern" for the E-Bb tritone pair with all the triads in the first inversion.

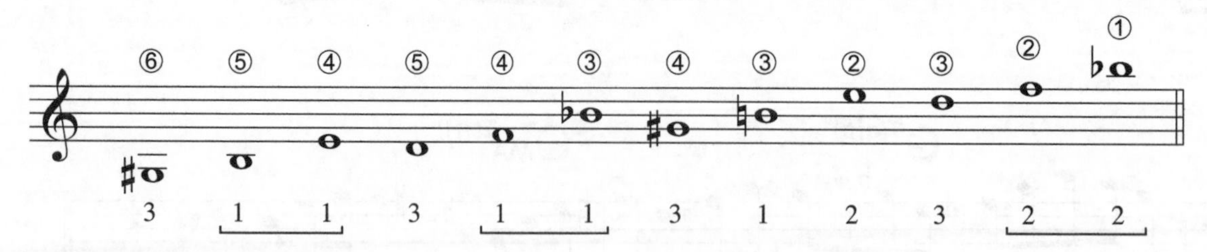

Ex.3-44 shows a "special pattern" for the E-Bb tritone pair with all the triads in root position.

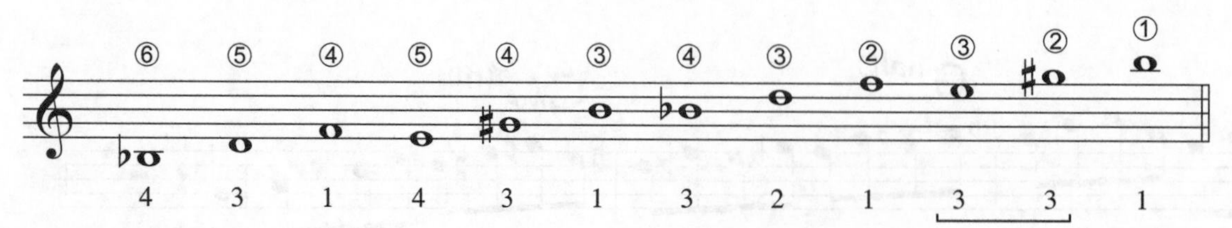

Ex.3-45 shows a "special pattern" for the E-Bb tritone pair with all the triads in the second inversion.

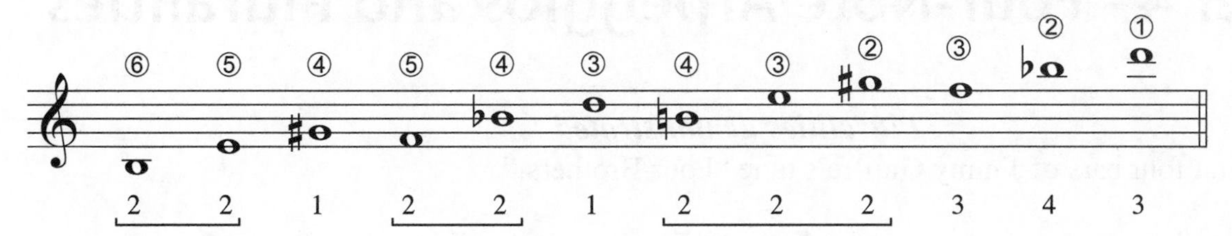

Work out as many fingerings and positions as you can think of.

The minor-major whole-step pair

Ex.3-46 shows a "special pattern" for a minor-major whole-step pair, which is a minor triad and a major triad up a whole-step. In this case the triads are D minor and E major. This pair can be used to create interesting lines for E7b9, E7susb9, Dmi6/9#11, and Fmaj7#9#11 among others (it can be found inside the A harmonic minor scale). Only this one fingering is shown. The rest of the work is up to you.

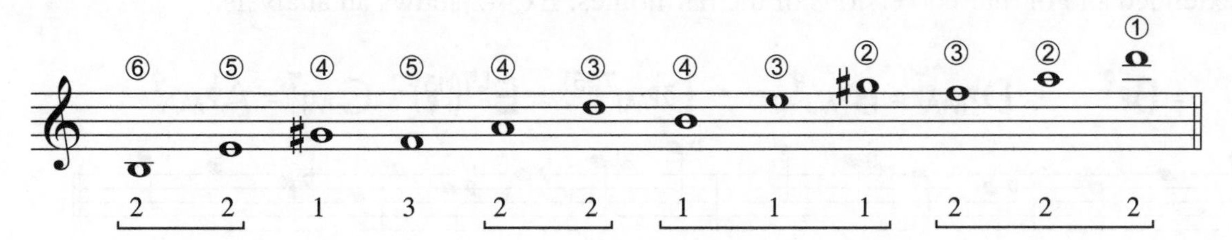

The minor half-step pair

The minor half-step pair is, as the name implies, two minor triads a half-step apart. Ex.3-47 is a sample line derived from the Gmi-F#mi half-step pair. Since no patterns were given, the strings and fingerings are shown. Try the line over Gmi-maj7#11, A13b9, A13susb9, Bbmaj7#5#9, and F#7alt9b13. The pair can be found inside the D harmonic major scale, a D major scale with a flat sixth (Bb instead of B natural). Hopefully this line might inspire you to search for some fingering patterns and more lines for the minor half-step pair.

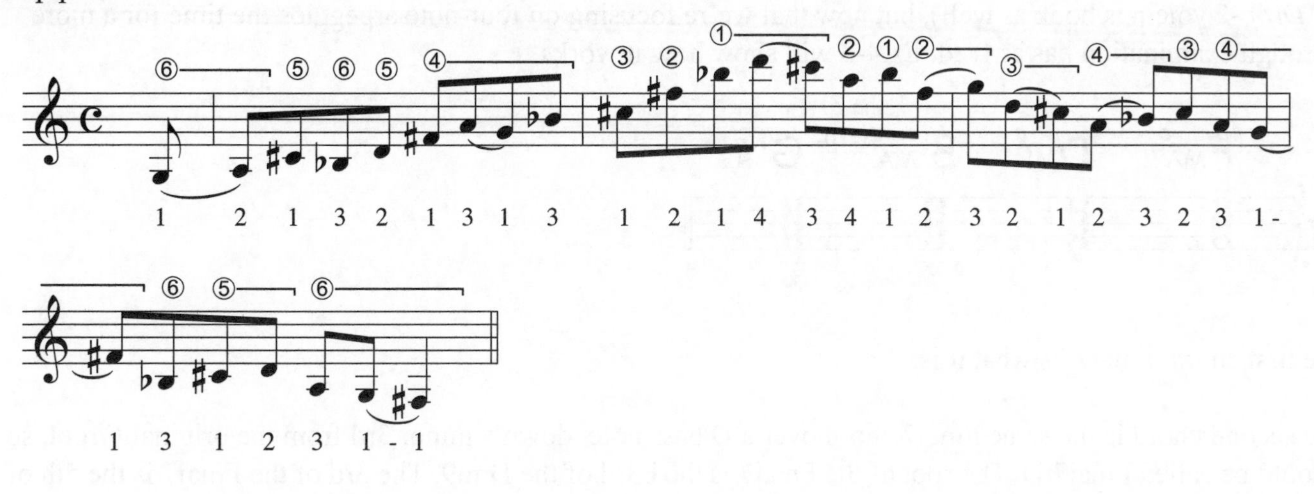

Chapter 4 - Four-Note Arpeggios and Pluralities

Pluralities demonstrated

Play ex.4-1, the first four bars of Jimmy Giuffre's tune "Four Brothers."

This is an example showing the application of the "pluralities" concept to four-note arpeggios. The actual arpeggios played are not the arpeggios of the basic indicated changes, but of other basic four-note arpeggios that imply more extended and/or altered versions of the harmonies. Ex.4-2 shows an analysis.

The Dmi7b5 arpeggio represents the 3rd, 5th, b7th, and 9th of a Bb9 chord. The Dbmaj7 arpeggio represents the b3rd, 5th, b7th, and 9th of a Bbmi9 chord. The next arpeggio has been re-spelled so it is seen to be a Dbmi7b5 arpeggio, representing the b7th, b9th, 3rd (the Abb is also a G), and the b13th of an Eb7b9b13 chord. The Cmi7 arpeggio represents the 3rd, 5th, 7th, and 9th of an Abmaj9 chord.

Pluralities explained

I'm sure you noticed that this pluralities concept has already been in heavy use throughout this book (and in my *Drop-2* voicings book as well), but now that we're focusing on four-note arpeggios the time for a more thorough examination has arrived. Ex.4-3 will show how it works.

The first chord, Fmaj7, is what it is.

The second chord is the same Fmaj7 chord over a D bass note, down a minor 3rd from the original F root, so it could be called Fmaj7/D. The root of the Fmaj7 is the b3rd of the Dmi9. The 3rd of the Fmaj7 is the 5th of the Dmi9. The 5th of the Fmaj7 is the b7th of the Dmi9, and the 7th of the Fmaj7 is the 9th of the Dmi9.

The third chord is, again, the same Fmaj7 chord over a Bb bass note, down a major 3rd from the previous D bass note. It could be called Fmaj7/Bb. The root of the Fmaj7 is the 5th of the Bbmaj9#11. The 3rd of the Fmaj7 is the 7th of the Bbmaj9#11. The 5th of the Fmaj7 is the 9th of the Bbmaj9#11. The 7th of the Fmaj7 is the #11th of the Bbmaj9#11.

The last chord is our Fmaj7 chord over a G bass note, down a minor 3rd from the last Bb bass note. It could be called Fmaj7/G. The root of the Fmaj7 is the b7th of the G13sus. The 3rd of the Fmaj7 is the 9th of the G13sus. The 5th of the Fmaj7 is the 11th (sus4) of the G13sus. Finally the 7th of the Fmaj7 is the 13th of the G13sus.

Time and space don't allow an in-depth analysis like we just did for every possible plurality. I'm going to show you a table that includes most of the popular pluralities used in modern jazz in one "key" for each. You'll have to do the analyses and all the transpositions.

Table of pluralities

Fmaj7	Dmi9	Bbmaj9#11(no3)	G13sus				
F6	**Dmi7**	Bbmaj9	G9sus	Ebmaj13#11			
F6b5	Dmi6	**Bmi7b5**	G9	E7susb9	C#7b9b13		
Fmaj7b5	Dmi6/9	Bmi11b5	G13	Esusb9	C#7#9b13		
Fmaj7#5	Dmi-maj9	Bmi9b5,11	G13#11	E13susb9	C#7#9b13(no7)		
F6#5	**Dmi-maj7**	Bmi9b5	G9#11	E13susb9	C#7b9b13(no7)		
F6/9	**D7sus**	Bbmaj13	Gadd9sus	Ebmaj13#11	etc. (see text)		
Fo7	Do7	Bo7	Abo7	E7b9	C#7b9	Bb7b9	G7b9
Fomaj7	Do9	Bo11	Abo7b13	E7b9(no7)	C#7#9	Bb7b9#11(no3)	G13b9

The chords in **bold** type are the basic four-note chords used for each plurality. Each plurality is horizontal across the page, with the roots or bass notes descending in 3rds. That's the easiest way to derive pluralities because tertian chords a 3rd apart share many common tones and easily substitute for one another. In general the basic chord is most likely to be at or near the left side of the table since it will usually represent the upper part of some larger structure.

The Fmaj7 plurality has a Dmi9 and a G13sus, which along with the Fmaj7 can all be found in the key of C major. All of the chords on that top line, including the Bbmaj9#11(no3), can also be found in the key of F major.

In the Dmi7 plurality all of the chords except the Ebmaj13#11 can be found in the key of F major, and all of them including the Ebmaj13#11 can be found in the key of Bb major. The F6 is an inversion of the Dmi7.

In the Bmi7b5 plurality all of the chords except the C#7b9b13 can all be found in the key of C major, and all of them including the C#7b9b13 can be found in the D melodic minor scale. The F6b5 and the Dmi6 are inversions of the Bmi7b5.

The Fmaj7b5 plurality has the same scale analysis as the Bmi7b5 plurality. I'm calling it Fmaj7b5, even though the note I'm calling a b5 is B natural, a #4. I'm calling it a b5 since there's no natural 5th and the B replaces the C in the voicing, so it's just a matter of practicality.

The Fmaj7#5 has an augmented triad in its structure, so it's not found in any major scale. All the chords in this plurality belong to the D melodic minor scale.

The Dmi-maj7 also has an augmented triad in its structure, so it too is not found in any major scale. All the chords in this plurality also belong to the D melodic minor scale.

In the D7sus plurality all of the chords except the Ebmaj13#11 can be found in the key of F major, and all of them including the Ebmaj13#11 can be found in the key of Bb major. When the D7sus arpeggio is played over the root of any of the chords shown, it creates the sound of the given chord symbol. The D7sus is very open, however, and can fit on top of many other chords without any clash, but also without defining the sound of the complete chord. Some examples would include C6/9, Ami11, F#7alt, C13, Cmi6/9, Ami11b5, F13, D7susb9, B7alt, and any kind of Gmi and Dmi.

The Fo7 has an eight-way plurality since it can come from the diminished scale. The diminished scale has no avoid notes so any one of its eight notes could be used as the root of a chord. Notice that four of the chords are all o7 while the other four are all 7b9.

The Fomaj7 can also come from the diminished scale, so it too has an eight-way plurality. The roots and basic qualities of the chords are the same as in the Fo7 plurality, but because the Fomaj7 is not symmetrical, the detailed names for each chord are slightly different from each other. It would be good for your brain to analyze each chord symbol to fully understand each name, but when it comes to actual playing you can keep your thinking simple since they work exactly the same way as the plain Fo7.

Even though there are dozens of chords listed in the table, there are only nine in **bold** type, and they are the ones we need to know to form lines over all the chords. Of course we'll need to practice the nine arpeggios in all keys and eventually know all the pluralities equally well in all keys.

Actually these four-note arpeggios are the same as what Mark Levine calls "four-note scales" in his books *The Jazz Piano Book* and *The Jazz Theory Book*. Since playing the four notes together as a chord always yields an ordinary chord, I've chosen to call them arpeggios rather than scales, but they are really the same thing.

Forms for Four-Note Arpeggios

Five positional forms

Guitarists should know at least five forms for arpeggios that lie easily under the fingers and go across the fingerboard in one or two positions. That will cover all the places on the fingerboard where the notes can be found with no gaps. Let's check out five forms in five different keys in the second and third positions.

Ex.4-4 shows one way to practice a Cmaj7 arpeggio in the second and third positions, with strings and fingerings shown. Practice the following forms in a similar way, starting and ending on the lowest note in the form.

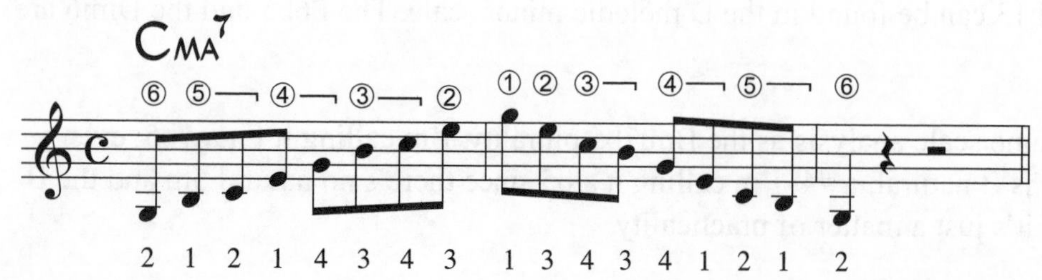

Ex.4-5 shows the form for an Fmaj7 arpeggio in the second and third positions, with strings and fingerings shown.

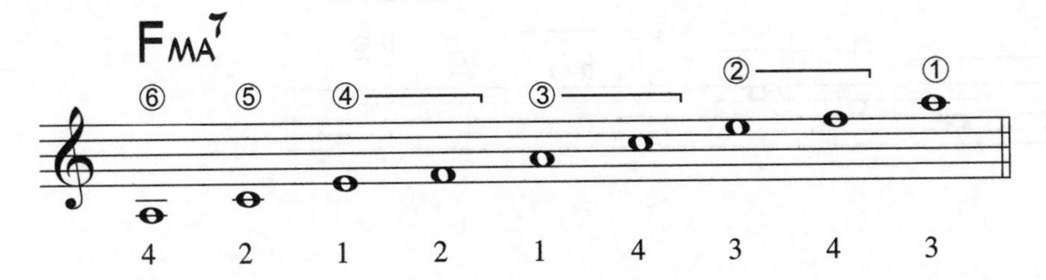

Ex.4-6 shows the form for an Bbmaj7 arpeggio in the second and third positions, with strings and fingerings shown.

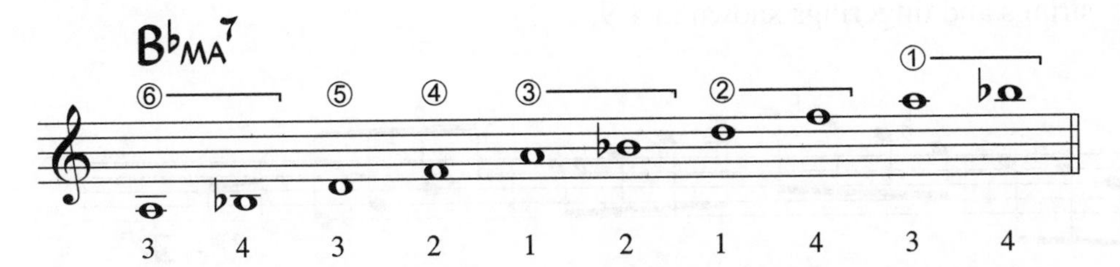

Ex.4-7 shows the form for an Ebmaj7 arpeggio in the third position, with strings and fingerings shown.

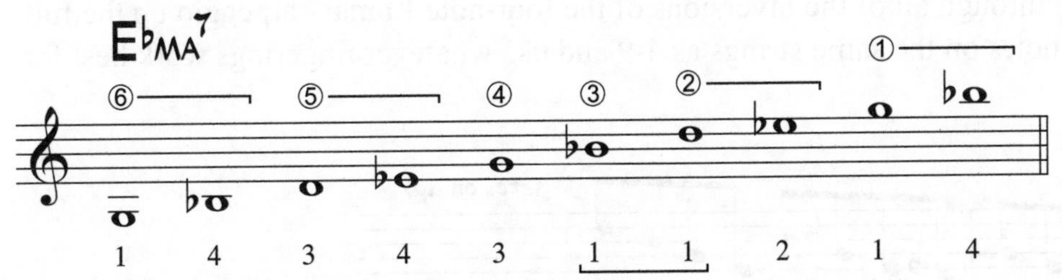

Ex.4-8 shows the form for an Abmaj7 arpeggio in the third position, with strings and fingerings shown.

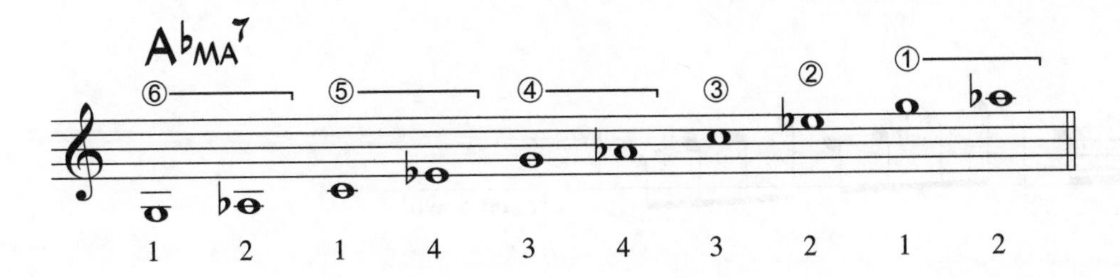

Converting the last two positional forms into long three-octave forms

Notice that the last two forms, for Ebmaj7 and Abmaj7, have two notes per string on the bottom two strings, totaling all four notes of the four-note arpeggios. We can use these user-friendly forms to create long three-octave forms. If you repeat the same four notes up an octave using the same fingering, but on the middle-two strings, then up another octave using the same fingering on the top-two strings, you'll get the long three-octave forms.

Ex.4-9 shows the Ebmaj7 arpeggio converted into a long three-octave form.

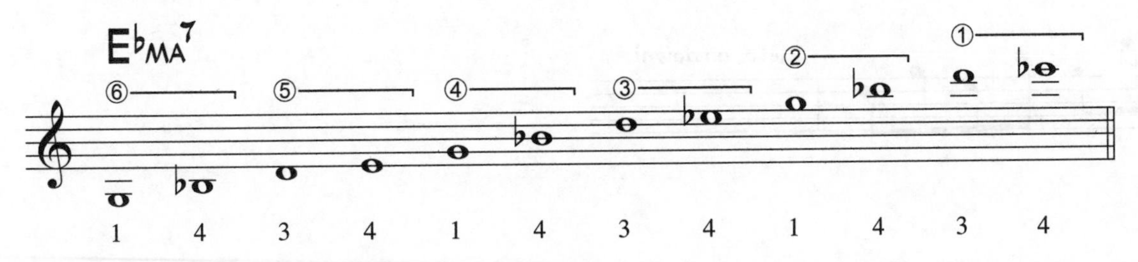

Ex.4-10 shows the Abmaj7 arpeggio converted into a long three-octave form.

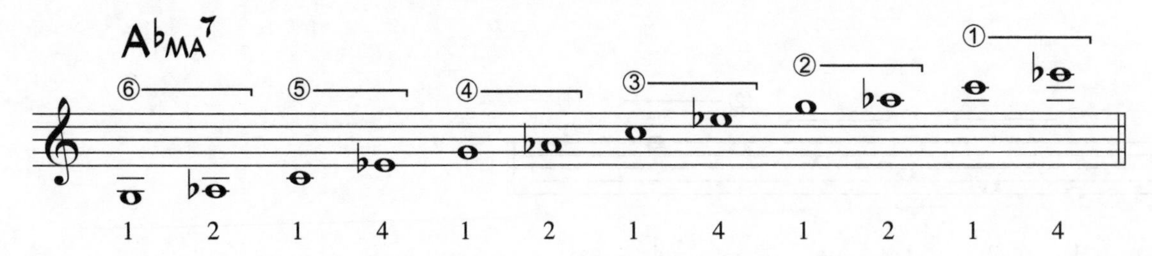

Some ways to practice the long forms

Ex.4-11 shows the long form of the Ebmaj7 arpeggio going from its lowest note up to the highest and then all the way back down. Use the strings and fingerings shown in 4-9.

Ex.4-12 shows a pattern running through all of the inversions of the four-note Ebmaj7 arpeggio up the full range and back down. Keep the notes on the same strings as 4-9 and use whatever fingerings work best for you.

Ex.4-13 shows a pattern that skips one note of the arpeggio. Again, keep the notes on the same strings as 4-9 and use whatever fingerings work best for you.

Ex.4-14 shows a pattern that skips two notes of the arpeggio. The same instructions still apply.

Ex.4-15 shows the same pattern as used in 4-14, but converted into triplets. This makes a more interesting cross-rhythm. The same thing can (and should be) done with 4-12 and 4-13.

All of the exercises shown in 4-11 through 4-15 should be applied to the long Abmaj7 form and all of the forms to follow.

The long mi7 forms

Ex.4-16 shows a long three-octave form for an Ebmi7 arpeggio, with strings and fingerings shown.

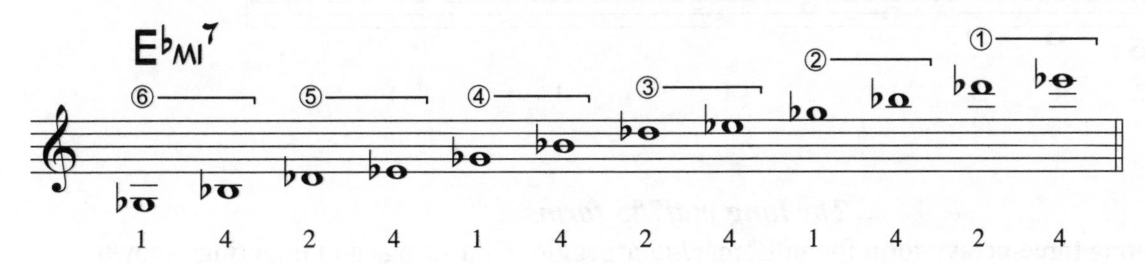

Ex.4-17 shows a long three-octave form for an Abmi7 arpeggio, with strings and fingerings shown.

The long mi7b5 forms

Ex.4-18 shows a long three-octave form for an Emi7b5 arpeggio, with strings and fingerings shown.

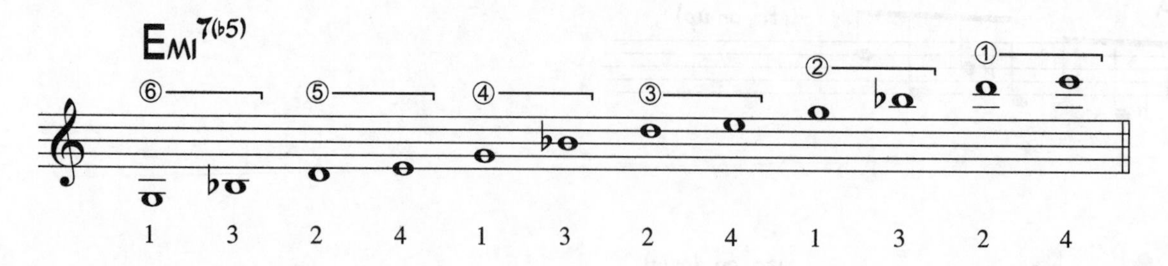

Ex.4-19 shows a long three-octave form for an Ami7b5 arpeggio, with strings and fingerings shown.

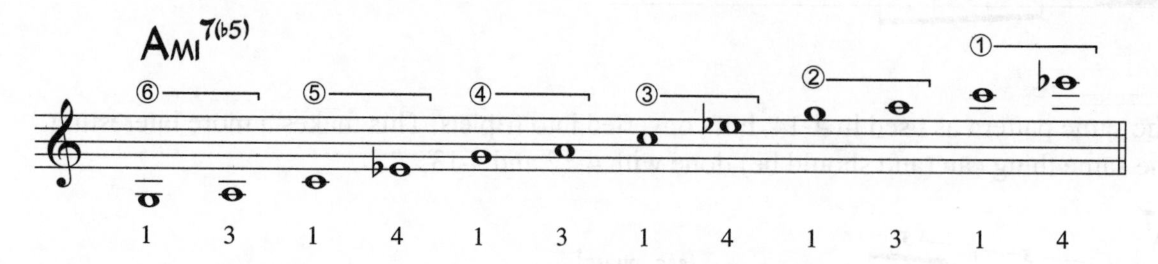

The long maj7b5 forms

Ex.4-20 shows a long three-octave form for an Ebmaj7b5 arpeggio, with strings and fingerings shown.

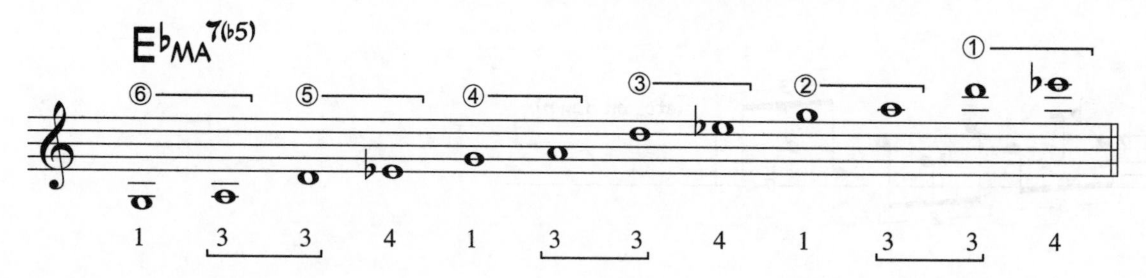

Ex.4-21 shows a long three-octave form for an Abmaj7b5 arpeggio, with strings and fingerings shown.

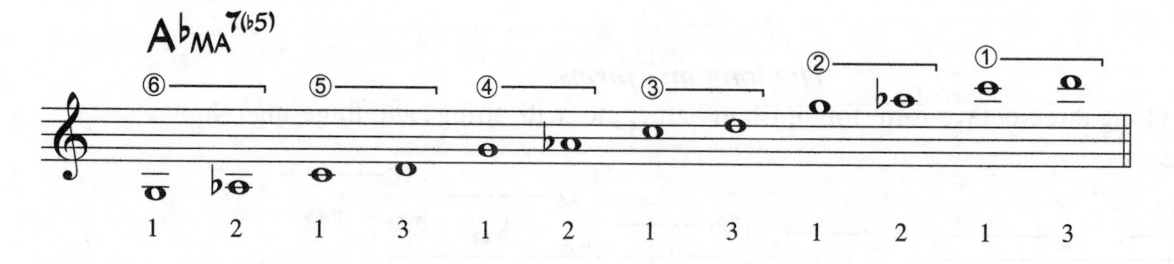

The long maj7#5 forms

Ex.4-22 shows a long three-octave form for an Ebmaj7#5 arpeggio, with strings and fingerings shown.

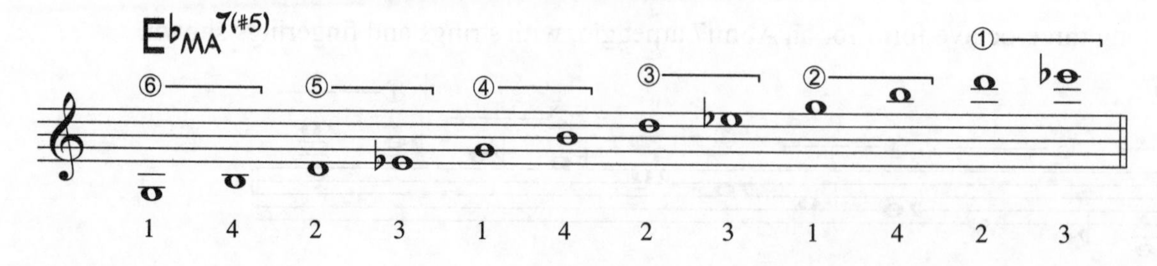

Ex.4-23 shows a long three-octave form for an Abmaj7#5 arpeggio, with strings and fingerings shown.

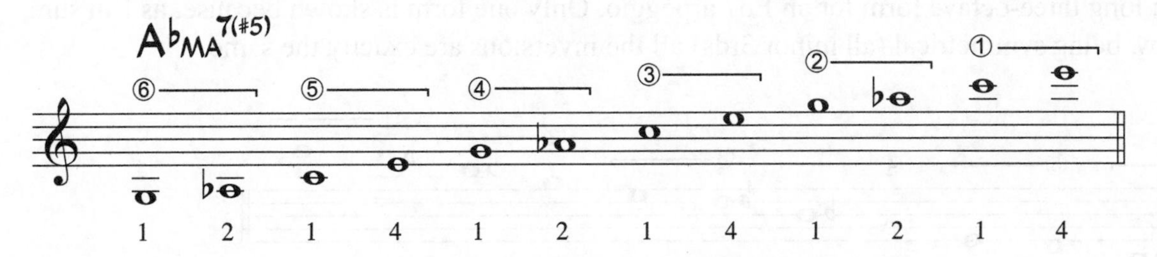

The long mi-maj7 forms

Ex.4-24 shows a long three-octave form for an Ebmi-maj7 arpeggio, with strings and fingerings shown.

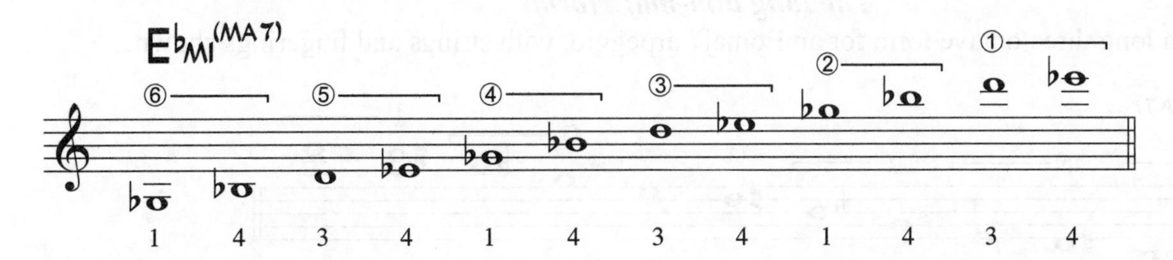

Ex.4-25 shows a long three-octave form for an Abmi-maj7 arpeggio, with strings and fingerings shown.

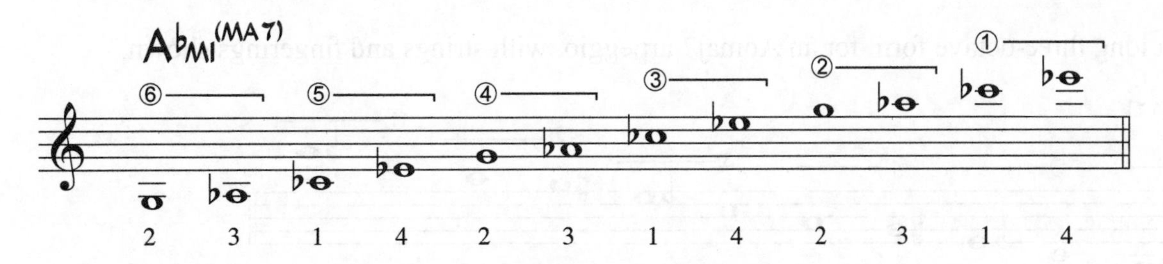

The long dom7sus forms

Ex.4-26 shows a long three-octave form for an Eb7sus arpeggio, with strings and fingerings shown.

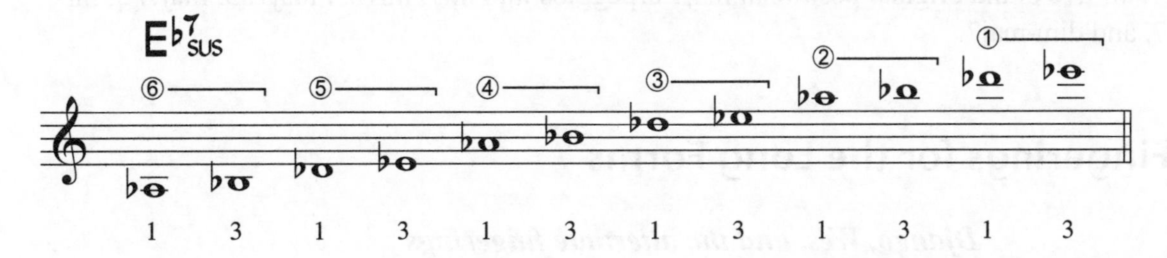

Ex.4-27 shows a long three-octave form for an Ab7sus arpeggio, with strings and fingerings shown.

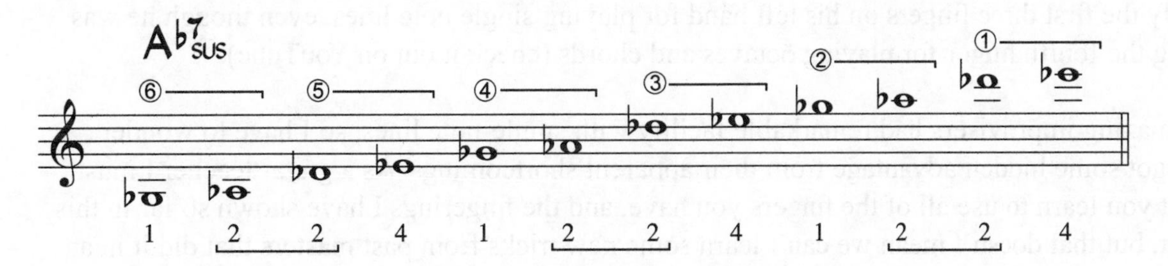

The long dim7 form

Ex.4-28 shows a long three-octave form for an Eo7 arpeggio. Only one form is shown because, as I'm sure you already know, being symmetrical (all minor 3rds) all the inversions are exactly the same.

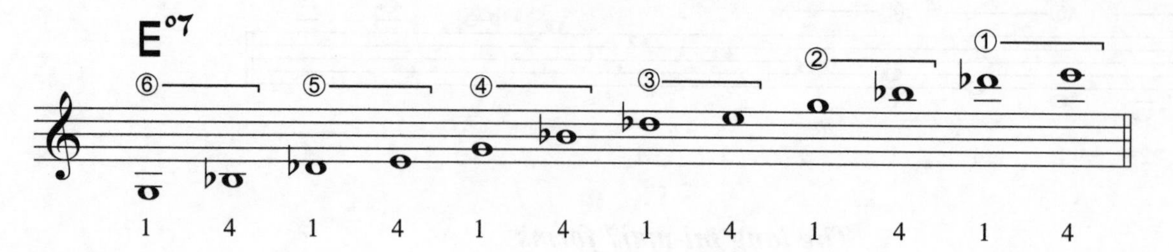

The long dim-maj7 forms

Ex.4-29 shows a long three-octave form for an Eomaj7 arpeggio, with strings and fingerings shown.

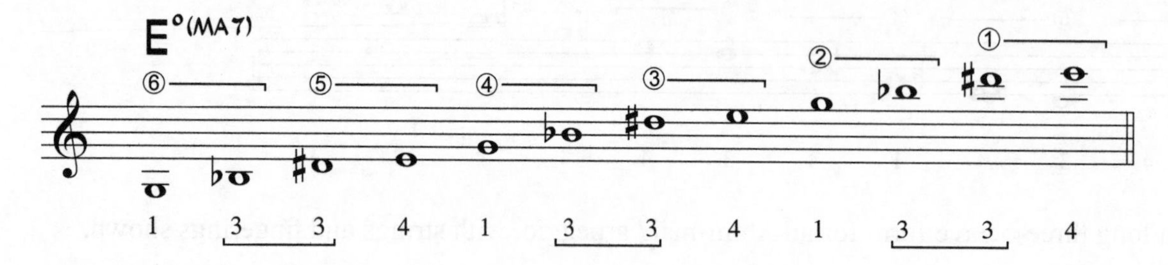

Ex.4-30 shows a long three-octave form for an Aomaj7 arpeggio, with strings and fingerings shown.

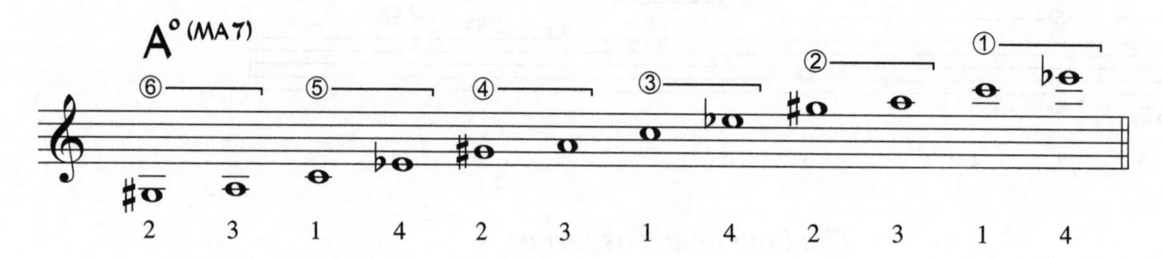

Of course convert all five of the original positional maj7 arpeggios into mi7, mi7b5, maj7b5, maj7#5, mi-maj7, 7sus, dim7, and dim-maj7.

Alternate Fingerings for the Long Forms

Django, Wes, and the alternate fingerings

Most guitarists know that a severe burn left Django Reinhardt with only the first two fingers on his left hand usable for playing single-note lines. Many guitarists, however, seem to be unaware that Wes Montgomery chose to use only the first three fingers on his left hand for playing single note lines, even though he was fluent with using the fourth finger for playing octaves and chords (check it out on YouTube).

Both of these amazing improvisers had remarkable facility with single-note lines, so I have to wonder if they actually got some hidden advantage from their apparent shortcomings. As a guitar teacher I must recommend that you learn to use all of the fingers you have, and the fingerings I have shown so far in this book reflect that, but that doesn't mean we can't learn some new tricks from past masters that did it in an unorthodox way (for an example of a contemporary master, check out Peter Bernstein). If you experiment with using only two or even three fingers you'll quickly discover that you can't really stay in a position for more than a few notes. You have to get comfortable with shifting the hand into different positions up and down the fingerboard, opening access to the entire range of the instrument in the process.

Since the long arpeggios we've been doing cover a three-octave range they require position shifts so they can be used to experiment with Wes-like and even Django-like fingerings. The forms shown above generally shift positions between the bottom-two strings and the middle-two strings, then again between the middle-two strings and the top-two strings. In the examples that follow the forms and locations of the notes on the fingerboard will be the same, but the fingerings will be user-friendly little groups that shift positions in various places to make practical two and three finger versions of the four-note arpeggios. In the forms shown above, not only do we use four fingers, but also frequently extended fingerings requiring long finger stretches. In the following forms with the alternate fingerings the concept is to shift the entire hand (including the thumb on the back of the neck) up and down to locations where the fingering is entirely stress-free.

Alternate fingerings for the long maj7 forms

Ex.4-31 shows the alternate fingering for the long Ebmaj7 arpeggio.

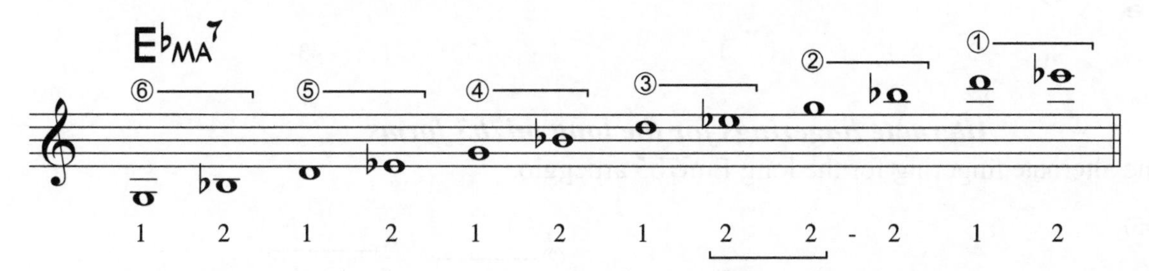

The first note is played in the third position. Then the hand shifts up to the fifth position and the next four notes are played there. This is followed by another shift up to the seventh position where four more notes are played. The top three notes are played in the tenth position. Of course practice all these arpeggios ascending and descending. This way of playing this arpeggio is "Django friendly" since it uses only the first two fingers.

Ex.4-32 shows the alternate fingering for the long Abmaj7 arpeggio, also "Django friendly."

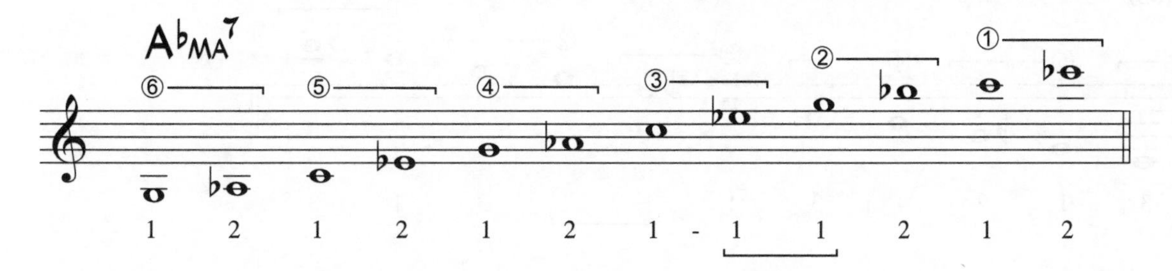

This time the first three notes are in the third position, then four notes in the fifth position, four in the eighth position, and the top note in the tenth position.

In all of the following alternate fingering forms except for the dom7sus and the o7, these same shift schemes will happen, so that when the root is on the fifth string, as in the Ebmaj7 form, the notes are grouped one, four, four, and three with shifts in between, and when the root is on the sixth string, as in the Abmaj7 form, the notes are grouped three, four, four, and one with shifts in between. All of the following arpeggios are "Wes friendly" since they use only the first three fingers.

Alternate fingerings for the long mi7 forms

Ex.4-33 shows the alternate fingering for the long Emi7 arpeggio.

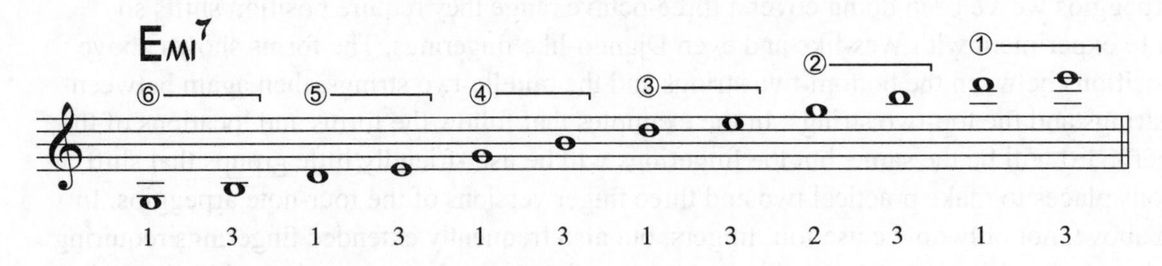

Ex.4-34 shows the alternate fingering for the long Ami7 arpeggio.

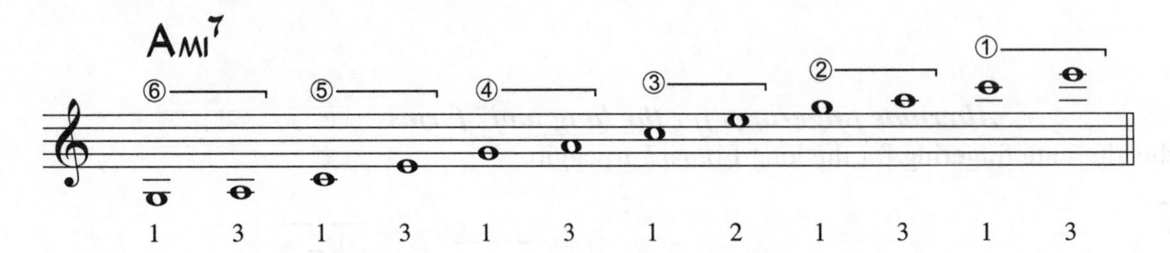

Alternate fingerings for the long mi7b5 forms

Ex.4-35 shows the alternate fingering for the long Emi7b5 arpeggio.

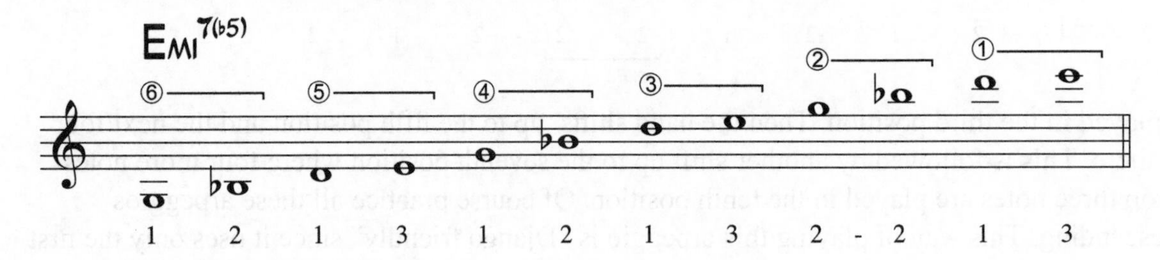

Ex.4-36 shows the alternate fingering for the long Ami7b5 arpeggio.

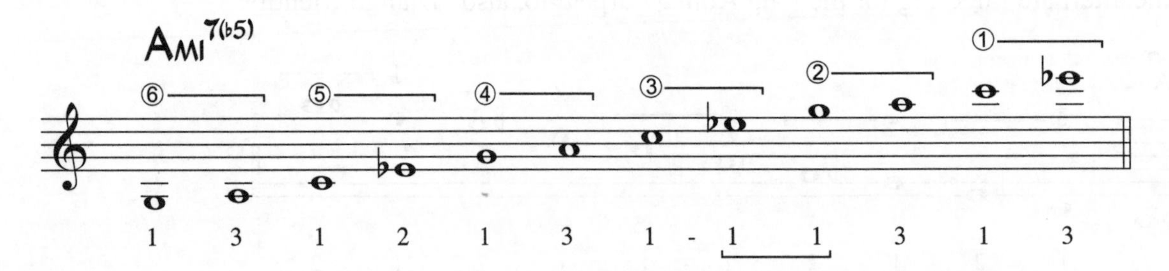

Alternate fingerings for the long maj7b5 forms

Ex.4-37 shows the alternate fingering for the long Ebmaj7b5 arpeggio.

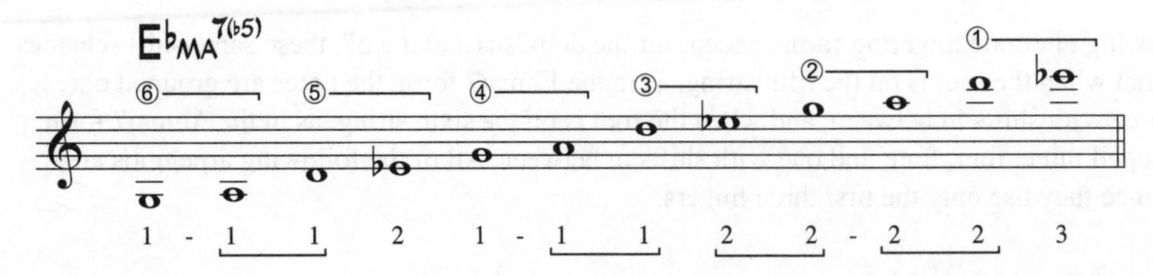

Ex.4-38 shows the alternate fingering for the long Abmaj7b5 arpeggio.

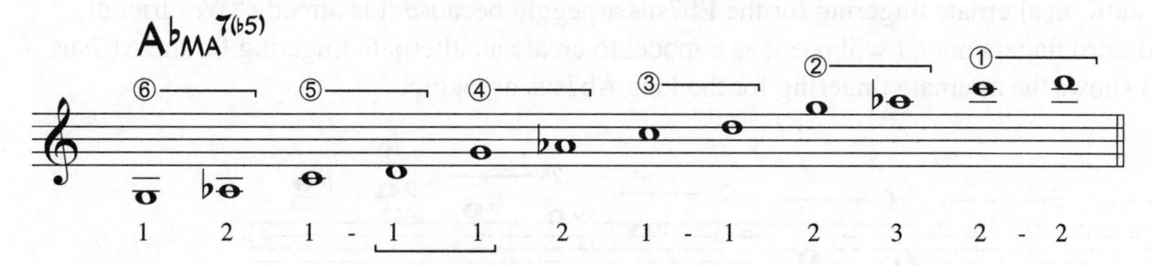

Alternate fingerings for the long maj7#5 forms

Ex.4-39 shows the alternate fingering for the long Ebmaj7#5 arpeggio.

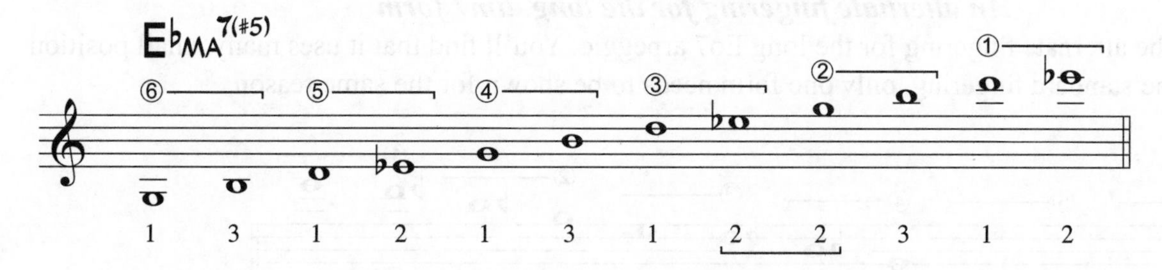

Ex.4-40 shows the alternate fingering for the long Abmaj7#5 arpeggio.

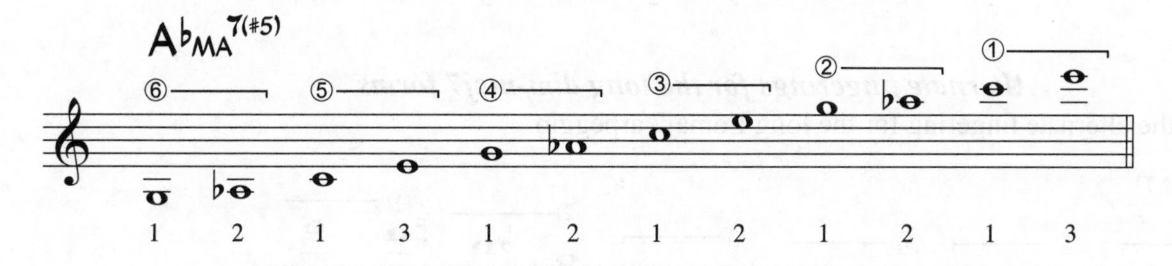

Alternate fingerings for the long mi-maj7 forms

Ex.4-41 shows the alternate fingering for the long Emi-maj7 arpeggio.

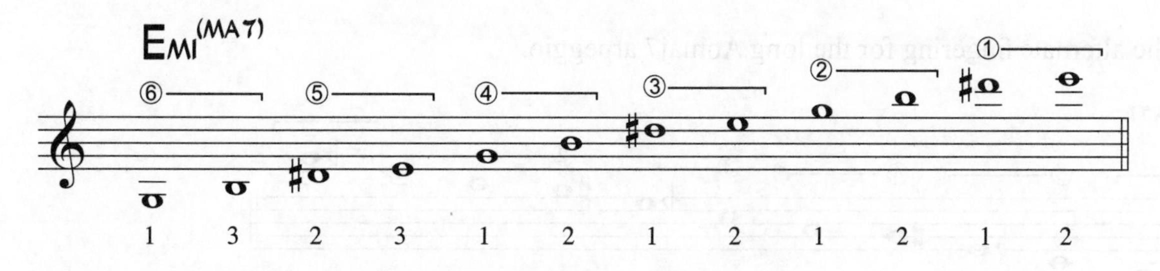

Ex.4-42 shows the alternate fingering for the long Ami-maj7 arpeggio.

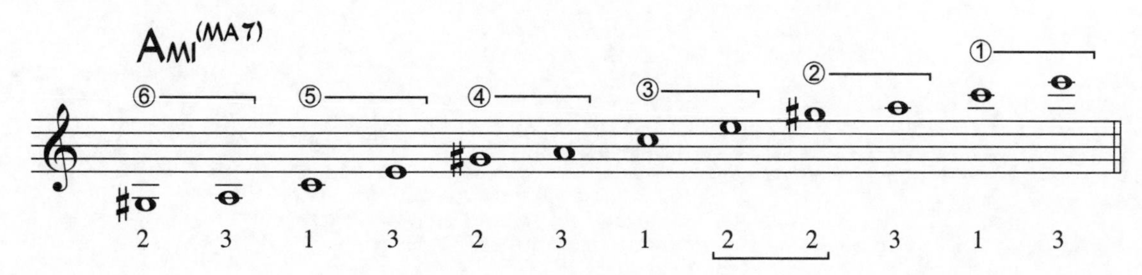

Alternate fingerings for the long dom7sus forms

I'm not going to show an alternate fingering for the Eb7sus arpeggio because it is already "Wes friendly," using the first and third fingers only. I will use it as a model to create an alternate fingering for the Ab7sus, however. Ex.9-43 shows the alternate fingering for the long Ab7sus arpeggio.

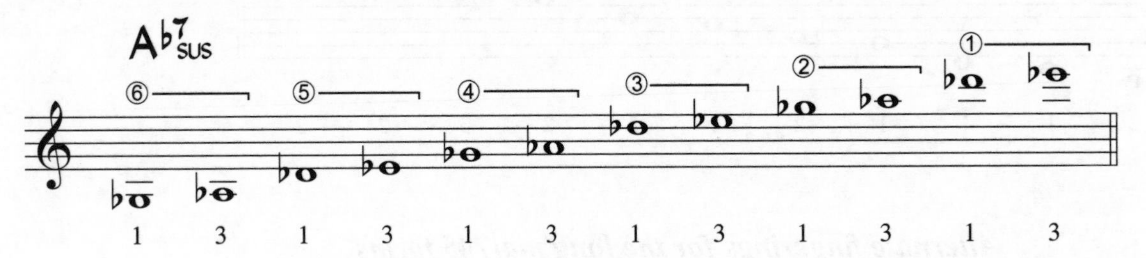

An alternate fingering for the long dim7 form

Ex.4-44 shows the alternate fingering for the long Eo7 arpeggio. You'll find that it uses many small position shifts. As with the standard fingering, only one form needs to be shown for the same reason.

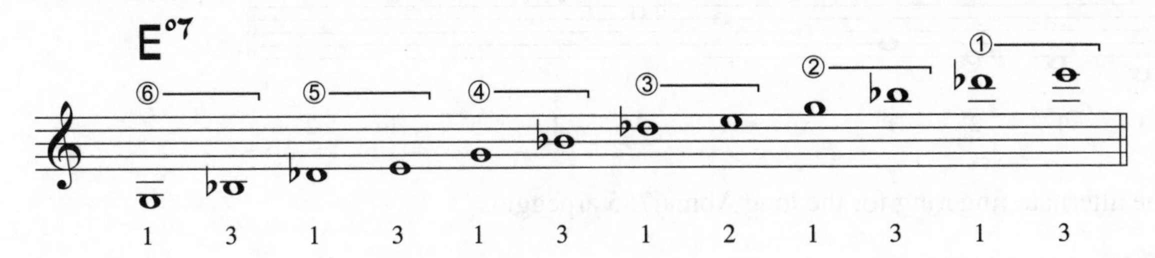

Alternate fingerings for the long dim-maj7 forms

Ex.4-45 shows the alternate fingering for the long Eomaj7 arpeggio.

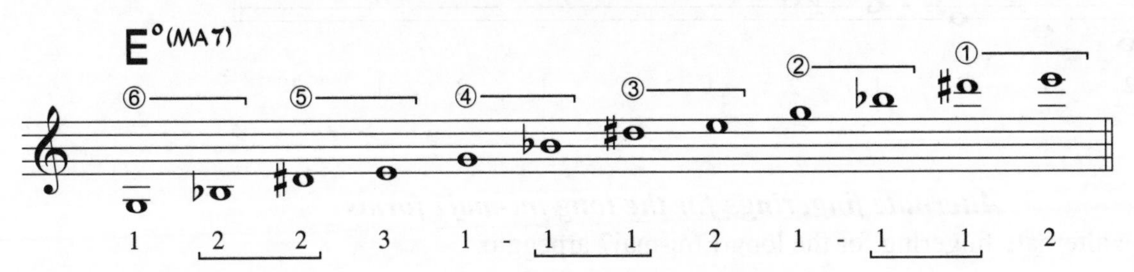

Ex.4-46 shows the alternate fingering for the long Aomaj7 arpeggio.

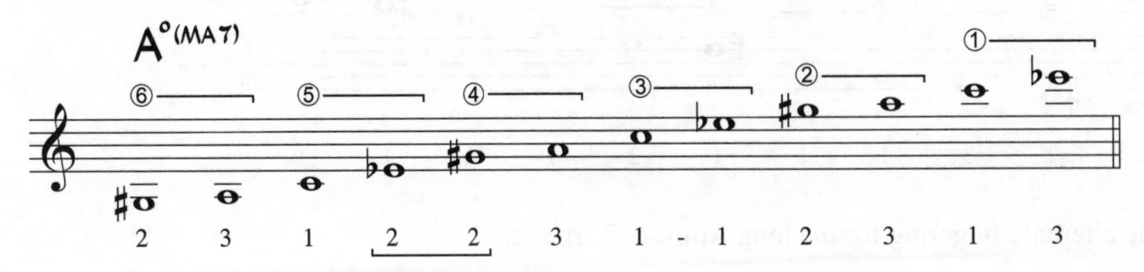

Applying the Four-Note Arpeggio Pluralities to a Standard Chord Progression

To demonstrate the use of four-note arpeggio pluralities I'm going to use the chord progression from the "A" section of a popular standard tune that all jazz musicians know. It's especially useful because it has both II-V-I in major and II-V-I in minor.

The progression

Here's the progression in the key of G minor: Cmi7-F7-Bbmaj7-Ebmaj7-Ami7b5-D7-Gmi6. The last Gmi6 chord has a duration of two measures. All of the other chords last for one measure each.

Selecting arpeggio pluralities to apply

Let's extend the Cmi7 to make it a Cmi9. If you refer to the table of pluralities you'll see a mi9 chord in the top line, a Dmi9. It's sound is created using the chord on that line that's in **bold** type, the Fmaj7. The Fmaj7 is rooted on the b3rd of the Dmi9, so to create the Cmi9 sound we'll use a maj7 arpeggio rooted on the b3rd of the Cmi9, the note Eb. So we'll play an Ebmaj7 arpeggio over the Cmi7 chord to define the Cmi9 sound.

Now let's extend the F7 using an altered extension to make it an F7b9. In the table of pluralities you'll find dom7b9 chords in the second line from the bottom. The process used in the previous paragraph can result in finding that an Ao7 arpeggio can be used to define the sound of the F7b9.

The Bbmaj7 can be converted into Bbmaj9 by using a Dmi7 arpeggio, and the Ebmaj7 can be extended to Ebmaj9 by using a Gmi7 arpeggio.

We'll extend the Ami7b5 to Ami9b5 using a Cmi-maj7 arpeggio.

For the D7, we'll extend *and* alter by using a Cmi7b5 arpeggio. Notice that in the table a Bmi7b5 can create the sound of C#7b9b13, so now we're just doing the same thing a half-step higher, using Cmi7b5 to define the sound of D7b9b13.

Finally, the Gmi6 is a tonic minor sound, so a Gmi-maj7 sound can be used. Here we'll apply Bbmaj7#5 to create a Gmi-maj9 sound.

Practicing the arpeggios ascending and descending through the progression

Hopefully you've practiced the arpeggio forms and fingerings in as many keys as range allows so you'll know various ways to play the following examples because I'm not going to show any strings or fingerings.

Ex.4-47 (on the following page) shows the arpeggios ascending for two octaves in eighth-notes on the first, third, fifth, and seventh chords in the progression and descending for two octaves in eighth-notes on the second, fourth, and sixth chords in the progression.

The Ebmaj7 arpeggio starts on the b3rd of the Cmi9 and ascends to the 9th of the Cmi9. Rather than leaping awkwardly to the root of the following Ao7 arpeggio, we go down a step to the b3rd of the Ao7, which is the 5th of the F7b9. Then we descend the Ao7 arpeggio and connect step-wise to the next arpeggio and continue to repeat the process through the whole progression.

Running some arpeggio pattern sequences through the progression

Ex.4-48 shows a pattern sequencing through the progression using only the notes from our arpeggio pluralities. I'll leave the analysis up to you.

I'm going to continue to use the same standard chord progression to demonstrate lines that move through several chord changes, but it's no longer going to be four-note arpeggio pluralities so it's going into the next chapter.

Chapter 5 - "Loose Ends"

In the tradition of Mark Levine, I'm going to have a chapter called "loose ends" that will cover topics that don't exactly belong in any of the other chapters but are important in order to give our Line Games a proper wrap-up. Each topic covered in this chapter could deserve a whole book, but we'll just touch on each one because we don't have space for several more books. However, we want to have a brief look since these topics will give us some insight into how to go from developing vocabulary through practicing the Line Games to actual improvisation using the vocabulary in real-life playing situations.

The topics will include creating arpeggio pattern sequences that run through several chord changes in a progression, using chromatic voice-leading to build long lines, using simple comp-style melodies as "skeletons" to build elaborate lines on, studying solo breaks by looking at examples from the masters, studying how to start a solo by looking at examples from the masters, and studying thematic development by looking at how the masters develop their solos using motifs.

Let's get started by continuing to look at sequences that run through the standard chord progression we were just working on at the end of the last chapter.

Running Arpeggio Pattern Sequences Through a Standard Chord Progression

Play ex.5-1.

Notice the similarity to ex.4-48. The arpeggio patterns that are sequenced through the progression are the same, but this time it's the basic arpeggios of the chords without using the pluralities concept very much. This gives the resulting line a slightly less jazzy more Bach-like quality. On the final Gmi6 the Gmi6 arpeggio is the same as an Emi7b5 arpeggio, so in a way it is a form of a plurality and its equivalent can be found in the table of pluralities.

It gets even more classical sounding if we use triad arpeggios of the basic chords as shown in ex.5-2.

Ex.5-3 shows another triadic sequence using the same patterns as 5-2, but this time it's a kind of triadic plurality where each triad spells the 3rd, 5th, and 7th of each 7th chord.

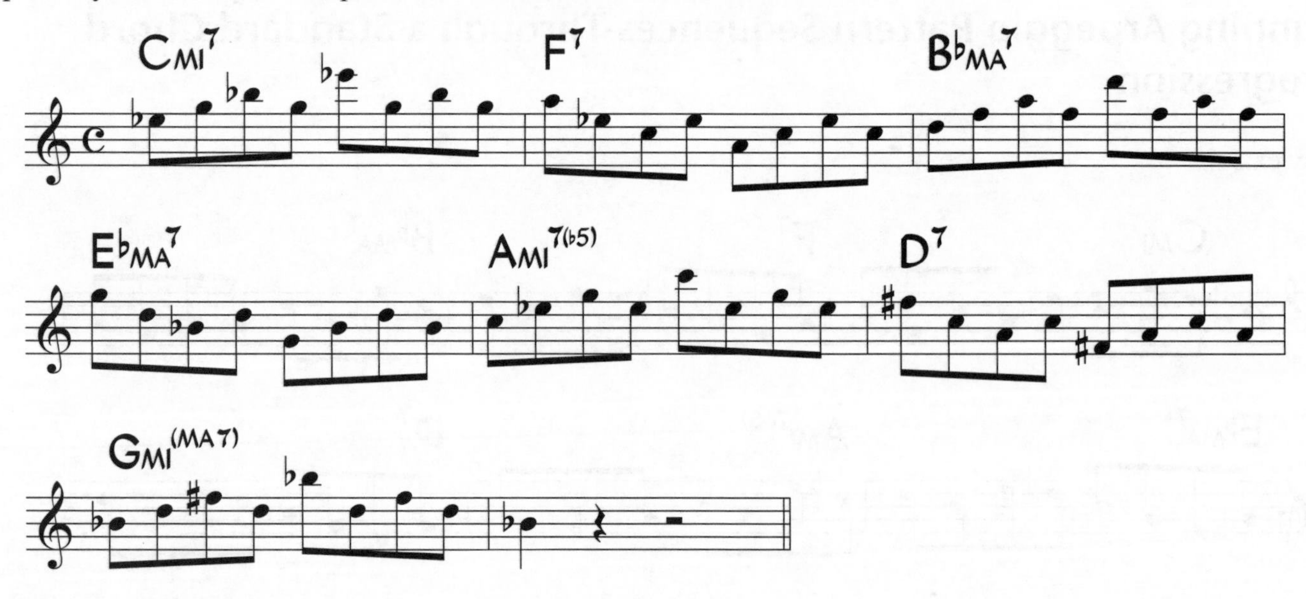

The first chord, Cmi7, uses an Eb major triad arpeggio. The F7 uses an A diminished triad arpeggio. The Bbmaj7 uses a D minor triad arpeggio. The Ebmaj7 uses a G minor triad arpeggio. The Ami7b5 uses a C minor triad arpeggio. The D7 uses an F# diminished triad arpeggio. Finally the Gmi-maj7 uses a Bb augmented triad arpeggio.

Applying basic triad patterns to another standard progression

Now let's apply some of the pattern sequences to the first "A" section of the popular standard tune progression used in ex.1-187 at the end of chapter 1. Ex.5-4 (on the following page) shows the basic triadic pattern applied to the new progression.

Notice how the sequence makes the line continue to develop in a logical fashion even when the key centers change.

Reversing the pattern sequence

Ex.5-5 shows the same progression using the same triad arpeggios, but the pattern sequence is reversed.

This type of reversal can be applied to all of the previous examples, and to many of the examples that follow as well.

Building sequences using patterns with added chromatic notes

Now we're going to use some patterns from the section in chapter 2 called "chromatically embellished triads" to build sequences that move through the progression used at the beginning of this chapter and the end of the last chapter.

Ex.5-6 shows a sequence using a three-note pick-up and diatonic upper-neighbor tones and chromatic lower-neighbor tones.

Ex.5-7 shows a slight variation of the sequence used in 5-6.

Ex.5-8 also uses patterns from the"chromatically embellished triads" along with various connecting notes to create another long sequential line.

These next sequences using added chromatics use patterns that that come from various parts of chapter 2.

Ex.5-9 shows one such sequence.

Ex.5-10 shows another.

I think that's enough to demonstrate how to play through longer progressions by using sequences, so let's move on.

Using Chromatic Voice-Leading to Build Long Lines

This section will show some lines that also have sequences, but they are organized by a new principle, chromatic voice-leading. Sometimes, if you use your imagination and look hard enough, you can find chromatic lines that can lead a voice through a long series of conventional chord changes. The notes in these chromatic lines can be used as the main focal points around which to build long elaborate phrases. I'm going to use the progression found in the first seven bars of a famous tune by Sonny Rollins that most jazz musicians know. The basic changes are: Ami7-D7-Gmaj7-E7-Ami7-D7-Gmaj7 (one bar each).

Finding a descending chromatic voice

Ex.5-11 shows a descending chromatic line that moves through the whole progression, except it becomes a common tone on the last chord.

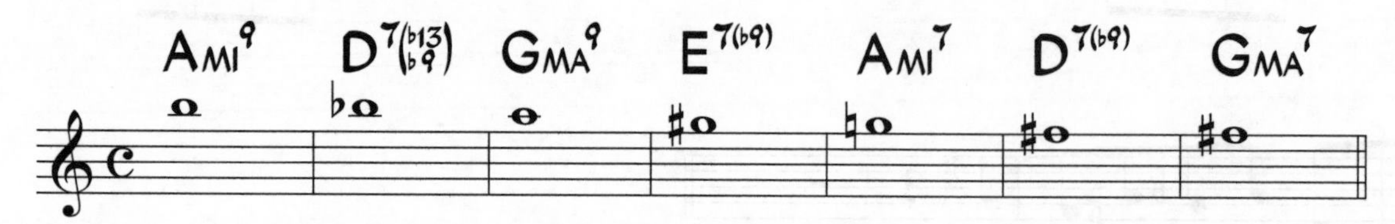

To create the chromatic descent we have to use some extensions and/or alterations. The first note, B, makes the Ami7 become an Ami9, while the second note, Bb, is the b13th of the D7, so we'll make it a D7b9b13. The A note creates a Gmaj9. The G# is the 3rd of the E7, but let's use an E7b9. The G is the 7th of Ami7, so no adjustment is required. The first F# is the 3rd of our chosen chord, D7b9. The second F# is the major 7th of Gmaj7.

Building a line around the descending voice

Ex.5-12 shows one possible line derived from the descending voice.

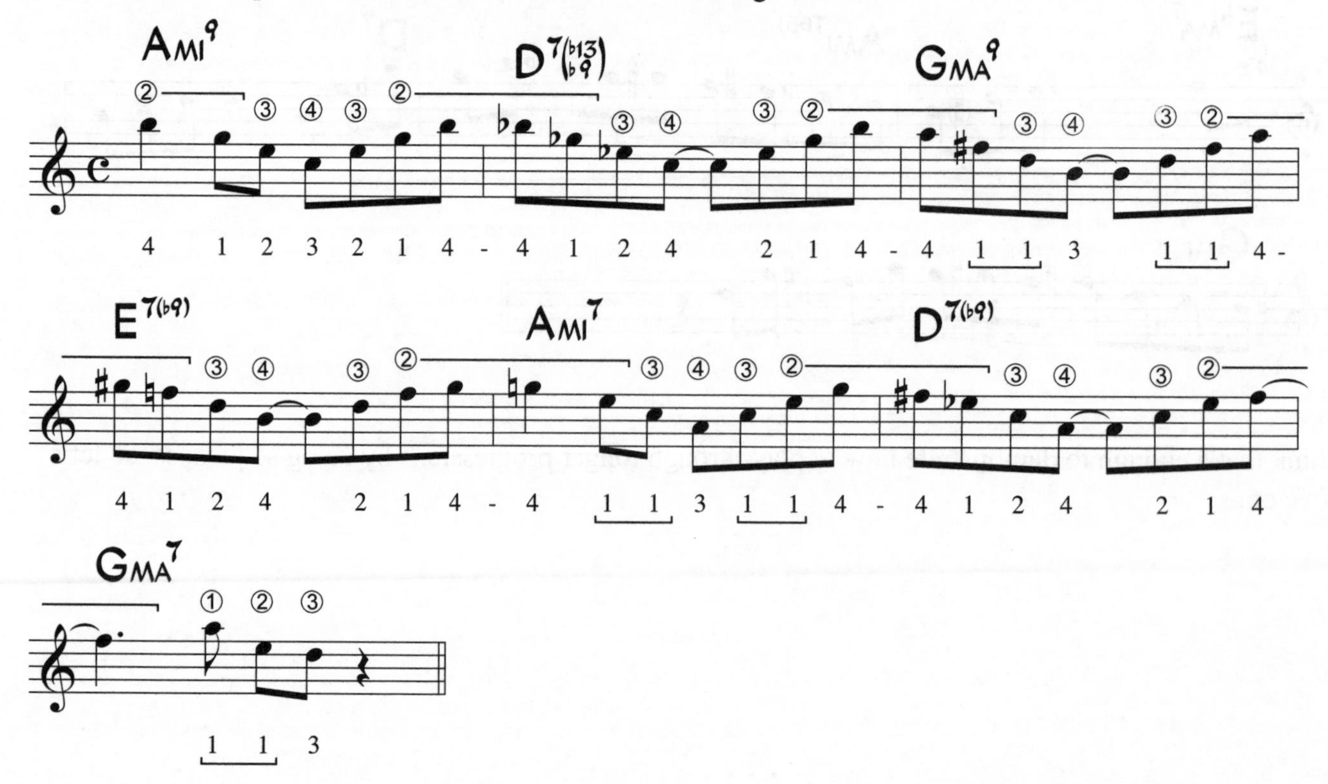

This line is dominated by four-note arpeggios. Since we're using several extensions and/or alterations, the pluralities concept is applied. The B note is the top note of a Cmaj7 arpeggio used to create the Ami9. The Bb note is the top note of a Cmi7b5 arpeggio used to create the sound of the D7b9b13. The A note is the top note of a Bmi7 arpeggio used to create the Gmaj9. The G# is in the G#o7 arpeggio used to create the sound of the E7b9. G is the top note of the Ami7 arpeggio. The first F# is in the F#o7 arpeggio used to create the sound of the D7b9. The second F# is the top note of the Gmaj7 arpeggio.

Adding a common tone to the descending voice

All of the chords in the progression are closely related to the key of G major. The fifth of any key is the most likely note to be usable as a common tone through a series of changes related to that key. The fifth of G is D, so let's see if it will work over the entire progression. D is the 11th of Ami9, the root of D7b9b13, the 5th of Gmaj9, the b7th of E7b9, the 11th of Ami7, the root of D7b9, and the 5th of Gmaj7, so yes it will work.

Ex.5-13 shows a line in half-notes that alternates back and forth between the descending voice and the common tone.

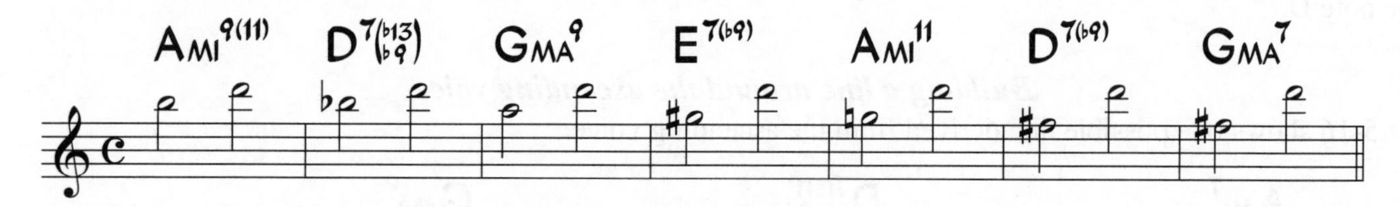

Building a line around the new combination

Ex.5-14 shows one possible line derived from the new combination.

It uses the same arpeggio pluralities used in 5-12, but also keeps returning to the D common tone, which acts like extra "glue" holding the line firmly together.

Finding an ascending chromatic voice

Cyclic progressions such as we've been using lend themselves to descending lines, chromatic and diatonic, while finding an ascending chromatic voice in such a progression can be tricky, but it can be done.

Ex.5-15 demonstrates one possibility.

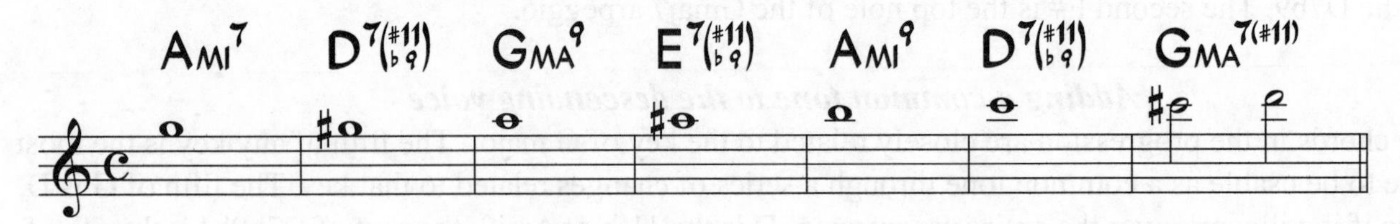

It starts on G, the b7th of Ami7, then goes up to G#, the #11th of D7b9#11. Next comes A, the 9th of Gmaj9, followed by A#, the #11th of E7b9#11. B is the 9th of Ami9. C is the b7th of D7b9#11. This leads up to C#, the #11th of Gmaj7#11. It could stay there, but I decided to show it going on up to the natural 5th of Gmaj7, the note D.

Building a line around the ascending voice

Ex.5-16 shows one possible line derived from the ascending voice.

The arpeggios used are Ami7, Aomaj7 for D7b9#11, Bmi7 for Gmaj9, Bomaj7 for E7b9#11, Cmaj7 for Ami9, and Abadd#4 for D7b9#11.

A slight variation

Ex.5-17 shows a variation on 5-16.

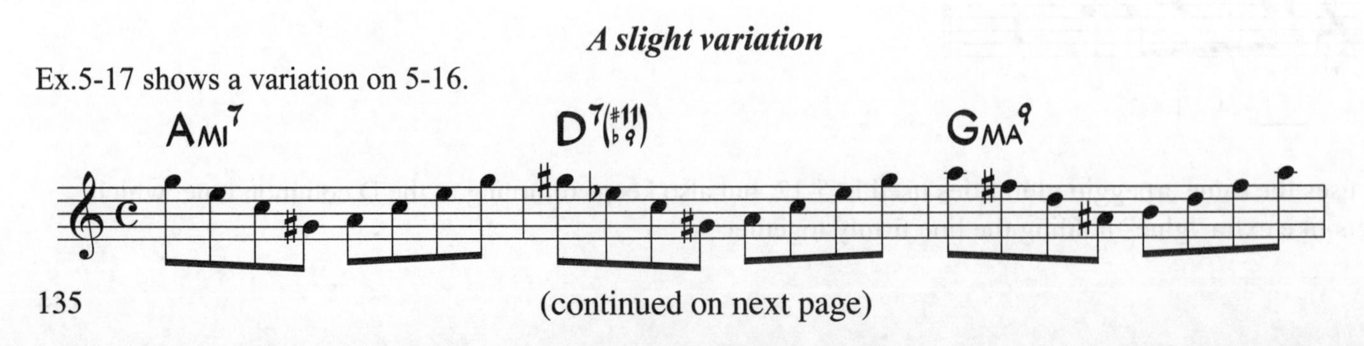

(continued on next page)

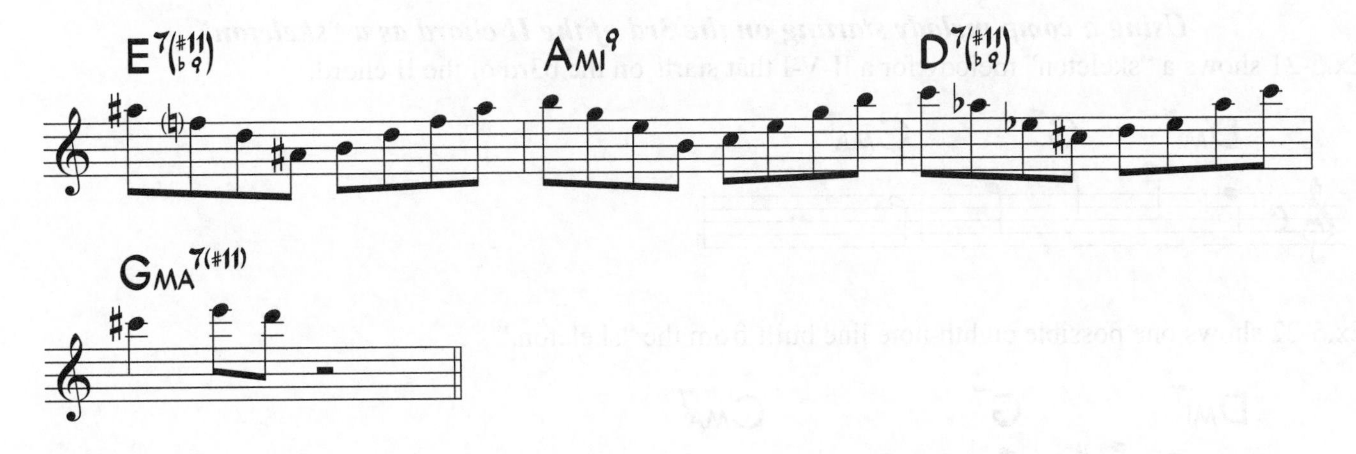

A few chromatic leading-tones have been added. You should be able to use the strings and fingerings shown in 5-16 to work out 5-17.

Building Lines on "Skeleton" Melodies

Actually all of the chromatic voice-leading based lines we just looked at can be thought of as being based on a simple "skeleton" melody, in this case a descending or ascending chromatic scale. This "skeleton" melody concept can use many other types of simple melodies to build from, not just chromatic or step-wise. For the top voice of chords used for comping, I'll usually try to form good melodies that are generally simple and inside, while avoiding too much chromaticism, so they could be perfect for demonstrating the "skeleton" melody concept. I'll use some II-V-I comp melodies from my *Drop-2 Book* (shown on p.31) to demonstrate. For many more comp melodies on II-V-I progressions in two major keys and in two minor keys, see my book *Three-Note Voicings and Beyond.*

Using a comp melody starting on the root of the II chord as a "skeleton"

Ex.5-18 shows a II-V-I comp melody starting on the root of the II chord as it appeared in *The Drop-2 Book*.

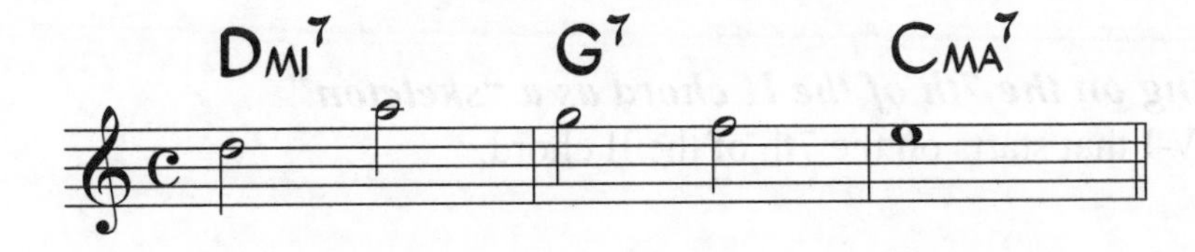

Ex.5-19 shows the same melody changed from half-notes to quarter-notes, making it ready to act as a "skeleton" for an eighth-note line over a short II-V-I progression.

Ex.5-20 shows one possible eighth-note line built from the "skeleton."

Using a comp melody starting on the 3rd of the II chord as a "skeleton"

Ex.5-21 shows a "skeleton" melody for a II-V-I that starts on the b3rd of the II chord.

Ex.5-22 shows one possible eighth-note line built from the "skeleton."

Using a comp melody starting on the 5th of the II chord as a "skeleton"

Ex.5-23 shows a "skeleton" melody for a II-V-I that starts on the 5th of the II chord.

Ex.5-24 shows one possible eighth-note line built from the "skeleton."

Using a comp melody starting on the 7th of the II chord as a "skeleton"

Ex.5-25 shows a "skeleton" melody for a II-V-I that starts on the 7th of the II chord.

Ex.5-26 shows one possible eighth-note line built from the "skeleton."

Using a comp melody starting on the 9th of the II chord as a "skeleton"

Ex.5-27 (on the next page) shows a "skeleton" melody for a II-V-I that starts on the 9th of the II chord.

Ex.5-28 shows one possible eighth-note line built from the "skeleton."

Using a comp melody starting on the 11th of the II chord as a "skeleton"

Ex.5-29 shows a "skeleton" melody for a II-V-I that starts on the 11th of the II chord.

Ex.5-30 shows one possible eighth-note line built from the "skeleton."

Combining the short II-V-I lines for repeated II-Vs and/or longer II-Vs

To make longer II-V lines you can connect two of the shorter phrases by selecting for the second phrase a line that starts on the same note that the first phrase would normally resolve to. Let's look at some examples that demonstrate.

Ex.5-31 combines the II-V phrases from 5-20 and 5-28.

The line from 5-20 resolves into the 3rd of the I chord, the note E. E is also the 9th of the II chord so we continue with the line from 5-28, which starts on the 9th of the II chord. Since the resulting longer line is made from two consecutive II-V phrases, it implies a repeated II-V, but can also be used over a long II-V with each chord lasting for a whole measure.

Ex.5-32 combines the II-V phrases from 5-24 and 5-30.

This time 5-24 resolves into G, the 5th of the I chord, but also the 11th of the II chord, and 5-30 begins on the 11th of the II chord.

Ex.5-33 combines the II-V phrases from 5-28 and 5-30.

Since 5-28 also resolves into G, it is also followed by the line from 5-30 played an octave lower.

Combining the "skeletons" into short II-V-Is

The "skeleton" melodies themselves can be sped up and combined to create more variations, using the same connecting principle used above.

Ex.5-34 combines the "skeleton" shown in 5-19 with the "skeleton" shown in 5-27.

Ex.5-35 combines the "skeleton" shown in 5-23 with the "skeleton" shown in 5-29.

Ex.5-36 combines the "skeleton" shown in 5-25 with the "skeleton" shown in 5-19.

Ex.5-37 combines the "skeleton" shown in 5-27 with the "skeleton" shown in 5-29 played an octave lower.

Creating different variations from the same "skeleton"

Of course these examples have shown one possible line created from each "skeleton," but many are possible. I'll use the "skeleton" shown in 5-27 to demonstrate two different possible variations.

Ex.5-38 shows a possible variation of 5-28.

Ex.5-39 shows another.

Look for variations for all of the "skeletons."

Creating and using alternate "skeletons"

I've only shown one "skeleton" from each starting note, but again many are possible. I'll show a couple of alternate"skeletons" starting on the 5th of the II chord to get you started.

Ex.5-40 shows one possible alternate "skeleton" starting on the 5th of the II chord.

Ex.5-41 shows one possible eighth-note line built from the alternate "skeleton."

Ex.5-42 shows another possible alternate "skeleton" starting on the 5th of the II chord.

Ex.5-43 shows a possible eighth-note line built from the new alternate "skeleton."

Minor II-V-Is and other keys

"Skeleton" melodies can be used to build lines for II-V-I in minor keys as well. *Three-Note Voicings and Beyond* shows comp melodies for all of the starting notes for II-V-Is in C major and F major and also in C minor and F minor, so it would be a good idea to try using them all as "skeleton" melodies. I'll show you the first two for the key of F minor, found on p.183, so you can see how it's done.

Ex.5-44 shows a "skeleton" melody based on the comp melody shown in ex.11-28 from the voicings book.

Ex.5-45 shows one possible eighth-note line built from the "skeleton."

Ex.5-46 shows a "skeleton" melody based on the comp melody shown in ex.11-29 from the voicings book.

Ex.5-47 shows one possible eighth-note line built from the "skeleton."

Solo Breaks and Other Ways to Start a Solo

The very first notes you play in a solo will make a first impression, so naturally you'll want them to make a good first impression. I've noticed that the masters always make a good first impression and frequently play something that seems to be inviting the listener to come along for the ride. In this section we'll look at some actual recorded examples of how some great improvisers began their solos. Many solos begin with one or more measures of pick-up notes leading into the the first bar of the first chorus of the solo. Often there's a solo break where the rhythm section stops and the soloist is briefly unaccompanied. Almost all solo breaks are pick-ups before the first bar of the form. Let's start by looking at some cool solo breaks.

Solo breaks

Ex.5-48 is from an early Joe Pass recording.

The tune is in the key of C major and starts on the I chord. The third through the seventh notes are a fragment from the famous "Gone But Not Forgotten-You're My Inspiration" quote, but rhythmically displaced by one eighth-note. Then Joe descends chromatically to an Eb, implying a G7alt going toward the C chord. A chromatic enclosure resolves convincingly to the note G, the 5th of the I chord.

Ex.5-49 is from another early Joe Pass recording and involves a quick two beat break.

The first five notes are the first five notes from the famous "Gone But Not Forgotten-You're My Inspiration" quote again, rhythmically intact this time. The break launches the nice two measure phrase that follows.

Four bar solo breaks are not as common as one or two bar solo breaks, but they happen occasionally. Tal Farlow recorded a nice one shown in ex.5-50.

It's a typical soaring Tal line that has many possible harmonic implications but lands nicely on the 11th of the Emi7b5.

Ex.5-51 is also from a Tal Farlow recording.

I've shown the measure before the two bar solo break because Tal brilliantly sets up the break by playing a "preview" fragment from the line he uses during the break itself.

Ex.5-52 is from another Tal Farlow recording.

It's in the key of Eb major and the form begins on a I chord. The interesting thing here is Tal's clever "sawtooth" line in the second bar. It bounces between the ascending chromatic line and the G note, landing perfectly on D, the 7th of the Ebmaj7.

Ex.5-53 is from an early recording by guitarist Rene Thomas.

This is a one bar solo break in the key of C major landing on the I chord.

Ex.5-54 also comes from Rene Thomas.

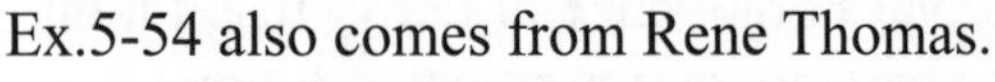

This one is a two bar solo break in the key of D major landing on the I chord.

Ex.5-55 is another from Rene Thomas.

This one is in F major and is two bars landing on the I chord. Rene Thomas' solo breaks are quite simple compared to the convoluted harmonic implications of Tal Farlow's solo breaks, yet they are still very attractive and inviting to the listener.

Ex.5-56 is from an early Wes Montgomery recording.

The tune is in the key of Db major and starts on the I chord. The chord at the start of the solo break is actually a Dbmi-maj9, and Wes' line reflects that. The Dbmi-maj9 is actually spelled with an Fb, but I opted to use the E natural for easier reading. Wes ascends and descends a C augmented triad to imply the sound of Dbmi-maj7. After descending to the Ab he goes down the whole-tone scale, implying Ab7b5. The line lands on the 9th of the Dbmaj7 before arpeggiating up the chord to begin the solo.

Ex.5-57 shows a nice two bar solo break that was played by Peter Bernstein on a recording by organist Larry Goldings.

This tune is also in the key of Db major but atypically starts on bIIIm7 that is part of a tritone substitute II-V for the II-V of V, followed by the II-V-I (figure it out). The chord at the start of the solo break is a C/Db and Peter's line leans on the G natural from the C major triad. The solo break is a string of eighth-notes that begins and ends off-the-beat, which Peter follows with four on-the-beat notes for contrast before ending the phrase with two off-the-beat notes. The eighth-note pick-ups are also followed with some thematic development. He uses a simple two-note motif, down a major 6th, and then plays it down a half-step in retrograde (backwards), up a major 6th, followed by a resolving idea.

Some other solo beginnings

Many times your solo will have to start without a solo break, but you'll still want to make a good first impression, so let's check out some other solo beginnings.

Ex.5-58 is also from Peter Bernstein from the same Larry Goldings recording.

Again notice the nice balance between on-the-beat and off-the-beat notes. Peter starts with a strong descending octave followed by silence, making a simple but powerful two-note motif. This is followed by a line that has subtle variations in its pattern-like structure and ends with a variation of the opening two-note motif, descending a minor 7th to answer the earlier octave.

Ex.5-59 (on the following page) shows the beginning of another Peter Bernstein solo from the same Larry Goldings recording again.

The balance of on-the-beat and off-the-beat notes is again apparent. Peter makes good use of an interesting rhythmic motif where a note is tied over the beginning of a beat, followed by notes on the last two thirds of an eighth-note triplet leading to a note on the following down beat.

Ex.5-60 is from an early recording by Wes Montgomery.

The first E note is actually the last note of the tune's melody, so the solo starts with pick-ups leading into the first bar of the form. Notice how the second phrase is the perfect response to the first phrase. Both phrases end with a triplet whose last note is tied over, anticipating the next beat.

Ex.5-61 is also from an early recording by Wes Montgomery.

This example is written using triplet notation throughout, while much of it is really just swinging eighth-notes. This is because there are so many triplets and Wes' swing on this track is very much in the triplet groove. It could be notated in 12/8, but that usually indicates something other than swing, so I've opted to stay in the 4/4 notation.

Wes opens with a nice ascending triplet arpeggio in the first bar that is answered in the second bar with a complimentary descending triplet arpeggio. Then the next two bars become a response to the first two. Wes uses a transposed variation of the ascending triplet arpeggio, but follows with a different answering phrase to further develop the solo. The fifth bar again has a transposed variation of the opening phrase, but this time flowing non-stop into a longer descending line to release the tension created by the ascending transpositions.

Pure genius. We could go on for days since almost all great solos will have a great beginning, but I think we've seen enough to get the idea. Check out your record collection. You'll find many more examples. Give them a listen and see if you can figure out what makes them work.

The examples we just looked at all demonstrated the soloists' abilities to create a sense of development by using motifs and their variations. You'll find that great improvisers use that same ability to develop their solos, sometimes all the way through, not just to make a strong beginning.

Thematic Development

Examples from actual Wes Montgomery recorded solos

Let's begin by looking further into the same Wes Montgomery solo we were just checking out (5-61). Ex.5-62 shows three bars from the second "A" section.

Wes continues to develop the theme of ascending maj7 arpeggios in triplets starting from the minor 3rd of each mi7 chord, but he takes it further than before. Notice that there's the chromatic II-Vs, Ami7-D7-Abmi7-Db7. Wes frequently uses melodic sequences in this situation, and also repeats rhythmic motifs as well, contributing to the overall development. The second II-V, Abmi7-Db7, is almost an exact replication of the first but down a half-step, except for the G natural, the #11th of the Db7. The phrase that follows resolves the tension created by the rapidly ascending arpeggios.

Ex.5-63 shows the entire last "A" section of the first chorus.

The tune has an "A-A-B-A" form. During the "B" section Wes played a long string of non-stop eighth-notes (and some triplets) that outlined a sophisticated set of substitute chord changes. It contributes to the overall development by providing a contrast to the "A" sections. Then Wes returns to the theme of ascending in triplets up a maj7 arpeggio from the b3rd of each mi7 chord and the b7th of each dom7 chord. The line also descends the triplet arpeggios from the 9th of each mi7 chord and the 13th of each dom7 chord. This theme works its way through the first six bars. In the fifth measure Wes creates a slight variation by going up a Cmaj7#5 arpeggio on the Ami7, implying the sound of Ami-maj9.

Ex.5-64 comes from a different Wes Montgomery recording.

This excerpt has a nice balance of triplets and eighth-notes. The eighth-notes are swung in a similar fashion as the previous examples, but the notation is simplified as it usually is in jazz writing. I'll let you do your own detailed analysis if you wish, or you can just play the example and revel in its satisfyingly beautiful development.

Ex.5-65 comes from later in the same Wes solo as 5-64.

Here Wes substitutes fast-moving chromatic II-Vs for the usual single long II-V, and, typical to his style, sequences the lines, including the rhythmic motif. Wes is again using the ascending triplet arpeggios going up from the minor 3rds of the mi7 chords, but he inserts some lower-neighbor chromatic notes and descends to the #11th of each dom7 chord.

Ex.5-66 is from yet another Wes recording.

(continued on next page)

In this excerpt Wes is playing over a chain of fast-moving chromatic II-Vs with a tritone jump in the middle, creating a very "twisted" set of changes to negotiate. The tempo is very bright and Wes sequences the ascending triplets again. Here he prepares each arpeggio with an enclosure or surrounding-note figure. I've shown the measure before the sequence and to measure after the sequence to give it some context.

Perhaps that's enough of Wes for now (actually there can never be enough Wes), so let's move on to some other players.

Examples from an actual Joe Pass recorded solo

Ex.5-67 is from an early Joe Pass recording.

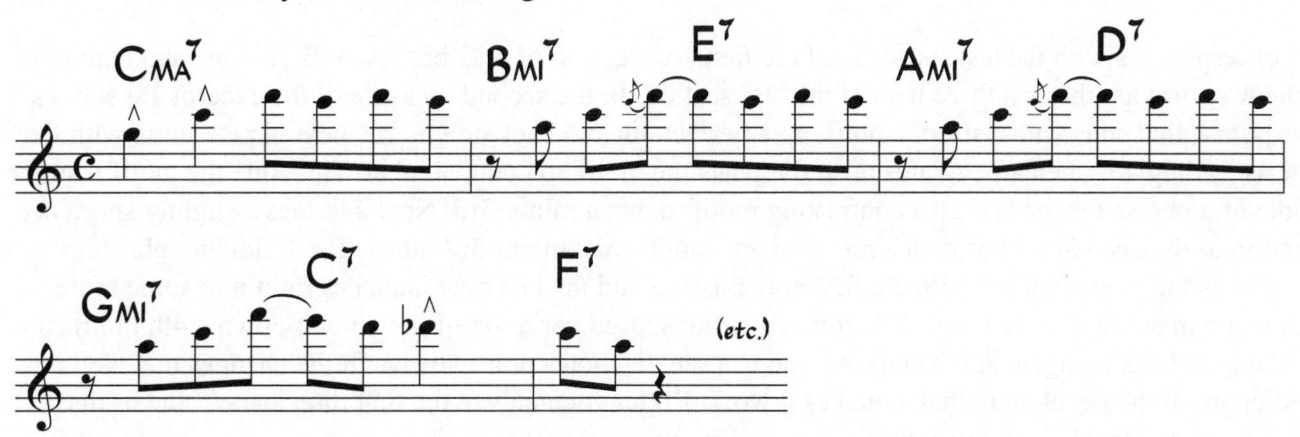

In this example Joe uses thematic repetition at the expense of the changes. Joe's theme and it's variations are strong enough to sail right over all the chord changes being played by the rhythm section.

Ex.5-68 is from later in the same Joe Pass solo.

This time Joe presents a simple ascending theme that he follows with a descending line based on the chord changes. Then Joe returns to the ascending theme and again follows with a descending line based on the different changes he's now playing over.

Examples from an actual Tal Farlow recorded solo

Ex.5-69 is from a Tal Farlow recording.

This excerpt starts with the last four bars of the first "A" section of a 32 bar "A-A-B-A" tune and continues all the way through the first three bars of the "B" section. In the second measure of the excerpt Tal starts a short phrase that ends with a simple motif: up a perfect 4th and back down. The next phrase starts with the same ascending 4th, then arpeggiates up and repeats the motif an octave higher. This time the motif is in the middle of a phrase that ends with a contrasting motif: down a minor 3rd. Next Tal does a slightly shortened variation of the last phrase but with a repeated and lengthened minor 3rd motif. The following phrase is the same as the preceding but with the first note missing and the last note launches right into some more contrasting material. On the Cmi7 Tal returns to a transposed variation of the up-and-down a 4th motif (this time he goes back up again at the end). As you can see, the notes don't always fit the changes that well but the strength of the developing theme makes it work. I'll let you analyze the first three bars of the bridge, where Tal starts developing a new motif.

Ex.5-70 is from later in the same Tal Farlow solo.

This excerpt starts with the last bar of the first chorus and continues through the first ten and a half measures of the second chorus. In the second measure of the excerpt (first measure of the second chorus) Tal ascends by a leap up to the the note F, arriving on the "and" of beat two. The next bar has a nice theme that lands on the minor 3rd of Gmi7, the note Bb, then leaps back up to F on the "and" of two again (the initial motif). In the next bar Tal returns to a slight variation of the nice theme that has one added eighth-note so it will land on the root of Ami7 this time. Then the motif returns, a leap up to F on the "and" of two. Next there's a variation of the nice theme that's been adapted to the D7 chord. In the ninth bar of the excerpt, which is the last bar of the first "A" section, Tal introduces a new theme that is three beats long. On the fourth beat he continues with a rhythmically displaced variation of the theme. Now the theme is adapted to the Fmaj7 chord. The B natural that ends the variation sounds suspiciously like an open B string, so it's impossible to be sure that the note was intentional and not a mistake. Each theme begins with a motif: a diatonic upper-neighbor tone followed by a chromatic lower-neighbor tone going to the target tone. After the second theme Tal returns to the opening motif, starting on beat three this time. Then he departs from the theme and uses the opening motif again, but transposed to fit the newly arrived Ami7b5 chord. The cross-rhythm created by immediate repetitions of the three beat long theme is most interesting.

Examples from an actual Rene Thomas recorded solo

Ex.5-71 shows an excerpt from a Rene Thomas solo.

The tune is a slow ballad based on the chord changes to a popular ballad that most jazz musicians know. The first four notes are a motif that Rene uses to create a strong thematic development. I'll leave any more detailed analysis of this example up to you.

Ex.5-72 is from later in the same Rene Thomas solo.

Rene returns to the same motif used in 5-71. The motif is strongly hinted at a few times in the first measure. Then starting on the second beat of the second bar the motif appears many more times with transpositions and also with rhythmic displacements creating a great cross-rhythm.

Examples from actual Jim Hall recorded solos

Ex.5-73 is from a Jim Hall solo on a recording by Paul Desmond.

The tune is a Bossa Nova and the excerpt starts from the beginning of Jim's solo. He wastes no time getting into thematic development. The end of bar one and the beginning of bar two presents a nice motive, a downward skip on two off-beat eighth-notes, which leads up the arpeggio, then to an ascending step-wise eighth-note line. Bar three presents another interesting motif, a downward leap of an octave starting on the beat, then staying off-the-beat as it moves up a step. This concludes the first complete phrase. The second phrase starts after the first beat of bar four with a transposed return of the opening motif, the downward skip on two off-beat eighth-notes. It's rhythmically displaced so the step-wise line happens right away, creating development through variation. Bar five is a transposed return of the motif from bar three. Bars six and seven start with an idea that is related to bar two, but the phrase is a significant variation to contrast the very similar themes of the first two phrases.

Ex.5-74 is from later in the same Jim Hall solo.

The opening motif begins with three eighth-notes that are pick-ups to the first complete measure. The rhythm at the start of the first complete measure echos the rhythms from bars three and five from 10-73, but this time it leaps down a major 7th and repeats the leapt-to note. The opening motif is then repeated, but with a variation. The pick-ups to the second complete measure have been changed to an eighth-note tied over to a triplet with an added chromatic passing tone. Next the opening motif is transposed up a perfect 4th with another variation on the pick-up notes. The following bar has completely contrasting material which then leads to a variation of the downward leap, an octave this time, but with the same rhythm and repeat of the leapt-to note. This is followed by more contrast with a similar melodic contour as the earlier contrasting material. Notice the similarity of the line on the Ami7 with Joe Pass hexatonic lines shown in chapter 1.

Ex.5-75 shows another excerpt from later in the same Jim Hall solo.

I'm going to let you analyze the details about this example. You'll find it to be a wonderful demonstration of brilliant thematic development.

Ex.5-76 is an excerpt from a Jim Hall solo on another track from the same Paul Desmond recording.

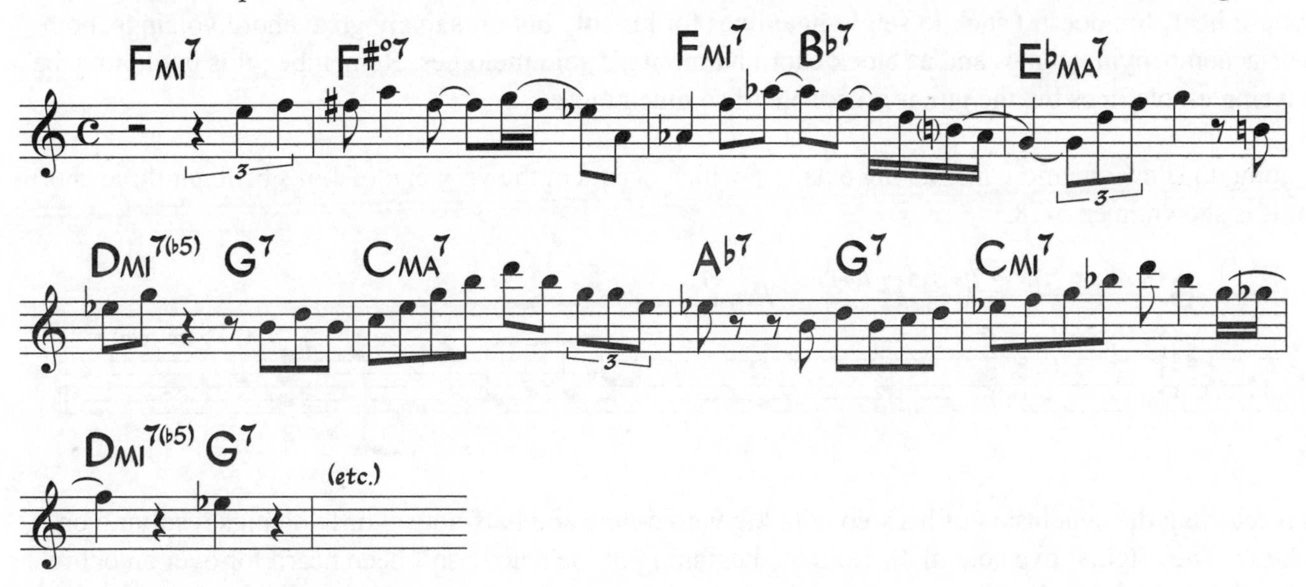

After the two pick-up notes in the first bar Jim plays a three note motif at the beginning of the second bar that he transposes down a half-step and repeats in the third bar, but displaced rhythmically. It starts on beat two of the third measure, creating a very interesting tension. The sixth bar has a phrase that ascends to the high D right on the third beat, then descends. The D is the 9th of the Cmaj7 chord. The phrase is mimicked in the eighth bar over a Cmi7 chord. Again the line ascends to the high D (the 9th of Cmi7) on the third beat, followed by a descent. These are just some examples of Jim's amazing ability to use motifs to develop themes and variations.

Ex.5-77 is an excerpt from another Jim Hall solo from his own trio recording "Live."

The excerpt starts from the beginning of Jim's solo. The first two measures are pick-up bars to the first chorus of Jim's solo. The five off-the-beat E notes create a tension that sets up the opening five note motif, the C-A-A-G-A. The next three bars are a response to the motif. Then the motif occurs again, followed by another three bar response that continues to develop with variations that follow the tunes changing harmonies. Next, you guessed it, the motif occurs again. I'm not going on any further but you should get the recording and give it a good listening because the use of the motif goes on and the thematic development throughout the solo is simply amazing. The motif occurs frequently in the first two "A" sections of the first chorus (it's an AABA form), then reappears toward the end of the last "A" section of the first chorus. The motif makes two more brief appearances during Jim's second chorus.

As you'll hear, Jim doesn't stick to single-note lines for his solo but uses many great chord voicings, both as self-accompanying comps and as block chord harmonized solo melodies. Remember, this book may be about single-note lines but the guitar is capable of so much more.

I'm going to show one more interesting example which occurs at the very end of Jim's brilliant three chorus solo. It is shown in ex.5-78.

Jim is reaching the conclusion of his solo with big whole-note and half-note chord voicings resolving on the Ami7. The original five note motif from the beginning of the solo hasn't been heard for over an entire chorus at this point, but Jim hasn't forgotten it and he makes sure his listeners haven't either by playing it again one more time, helping to give the entire solo a highly compositional structure. Pure genius!

I think that studying actual recorded examples such as these is the best way to get some real insight as to how to go about using thematic development in your own playing. I'm sure you can find many more examples from your favorite recordings.

I think that wraps it up for now. Good luck in your musical endeavors!

EPILOGUE – Introduction to "Cellular" Improvisation

This Epilogue is a sneak preview of topics to be thoroughly covered in a future volume. First let's explore "cellular" improvisation as a concept in itself. As you probably know, we have already been using many two-note, three-note, four-note, and occasionally five-note cells throughout much of this book. Actually, almost any long line of notes could be sliced up into short melodic cells which can be used separately and re-combined into other long lines. When jazz musicians refer to melodic cells, they are most commonly four-note cells. Hal Galper in his great book *Forward Motion* defines a cell as a four-note group with at least three chord tones. Jerry Bergonzi uses a similar concept.

Four-note cells are not only useful for re-combining into long lines over a given chord, but are especially useful for improvising lines over very fast-moving changes. Four note cells played as all eighth-notes last for only two beats, so changes that last for only two beats each are perfect for some cellular work-outs. These could include fast-moving cycles, quick II-V sequences, various turnarounds, "Coltrane changes" (as in "Giant Steps") and more.

Fast-Moving Dominant Cycles

A dominant cycle is a progression of all dominant 7th type chords moving counter-clockwise around the the circle of fifths (each new root being down-a-fifth or up-a-fourth from the previous root). Right now we want to check out changes lasting only two beats each, so we'll specify them as "fast-moving" dominant cycles.

Some actual examples of fast-moving dominant cycles

Play ex. E-1, from a recording of an improvised solo by Joe Pass. Notice that each cell begins on the root of each chord.

Ex. E-2 is also from Joe. Each cell begins on the 3rd of each chord.

"Root to root" cycles – one bar sequences

Ex. E-3 (on the following page) shows a "root to root" cycle using one ascending 1-2-3-5 cell followed by one descending 1-b7-6-5 cell, forming a one measure pattern that sequences down the fingerboard along the first two strings. Only the first two bars are shown. Continue the exercise as far down as practical.

The sequence shown starts high on the fingerboard, leaving room to work the pattern down the neck. During the course of an actual improvisation you may have to start a cycle much lower on the fingerboard. By combining different fingerings that will be shown in the upcoming book you can work the one bar sequence down across the strings, as shown in ex. E-4.

"3rd to 3rd" cycles – one bar sequences

Ex. E-5 shows a "3rd to 3rd" cycle, a one measure pattern that sequences down the fingerboard along the first two strings. Only the first two bars are shown. Continue the exercise as far down as practical.

By combining the different "3rd to 3rd" fingerings shown in the upcoming book you can work the one bar sequence down across the strings, as shown in ex. E-6.

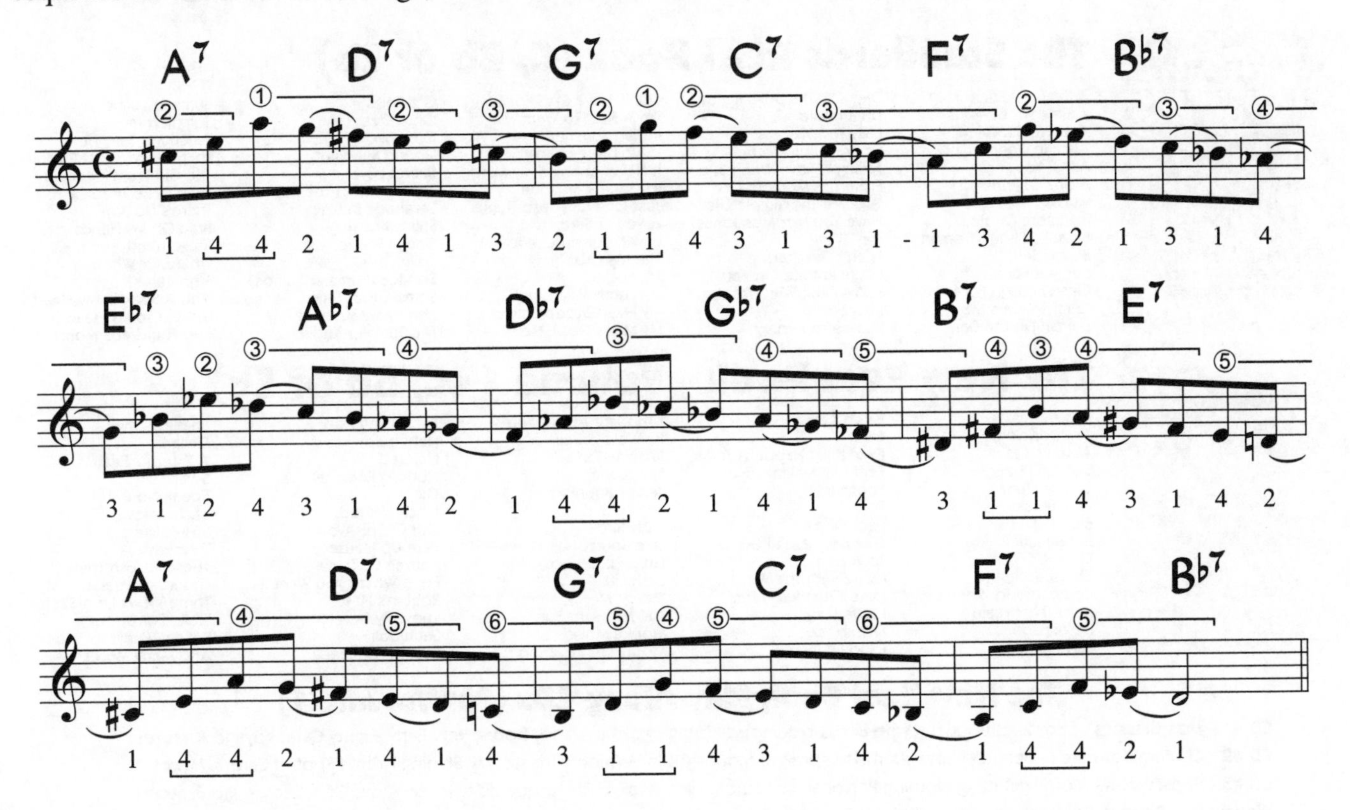

Other Topics

Of course this is just a tiny sampling. The next book covers cycles quite thoroughly, including II-V whole-step sequences and chromatic II-Vs. This leads into a comprehensive study of a wide variety of turnarounds, including what jazzers call the "Dameron turnaround," as well as "C.T.A." and "Coltrane Changes." These are followed by showing how to combine four-note cells into lines over changes of longer duration, such as long II-Vs and the Rhythm Changes bridge. Cells can be used quite effectively for playing "outside" of the given changes or mode and for "free" improvisation, all thoroughly covered. Side-slipping and intervallic cellular sequencing are also included. Finally there is an in-depth presentation of chromatic interval studies, serial tone-rows and 23rd chords.

SHER MUSIC CO. – The finest in Jazz & Latin Publications

THE NEW REAL BOOK SERIES

The Standards Real Book (C, Bb or Eb)

A Beautiful Friendship
A Time For Love
Ain't No Sunshine
Alice In Wonderland
All Of You
Alone Together
At Last
Baltimore Oriole
Bess, You Is My Woman
Bluesette
But Not For Me
Close Enough For Love
Crazy He Calls Me
Dancing In The Dark
Days Of Wine And Roses
Dreamsville
Easy To Love
Embraceable You
Falling In Love With Love
From This Moment On
Give Me The Simple Life
Have You Met Miss Jones?
Hey There
I Can't Get Started
I Concentrate On You
I Cover The Waterfront
I Love You
I Loves You Porgy
I Only Have Eyes For You
I'm A Fool To Want You
Indian Summer
It Ain't Necessarily So
It Never Entered My Mind
It's You Or No One
Just One Of Those Things
Love For Sale
Lover, Come Back To Me
The Man I Love
Mr. Lucky
My Funny Valentine
My Heart Stood Still
My Man's Gone Now
Old Folks
On A Clear Day
Our Love Is Here To Stay
'Round Midnight
Secret Love
September In The Rain
Serenade In Blue
Shiny Stockings
Since I Fell For You
So In Love
So Nice (Summer Samba)
Some Other Time
Stormy Weather
The Summer Knows
Summer Night
Summertime
Teach Me Tonight
That Sunday, That Summer
The Girl From Ipanema
Then I'll Be Tired Of You
There's No You
Time On My Hands
'Tis Autumn
Where Or When
Who Cares?
With A Song In My Heart
You Go To My Head
And Hundreds More!

The New Real Book - Volume 1 (C, Bb or Eb)

Angel Eyes
Anthropology
Autumn Leaves
Beautiful Love
Bernie's Tune
Blue Bossa
Blue Daniel
But Beautiful
Chain Of Fools
Chelsea Bridge
Compared To What
Darn That Dream
Desafinado
Early Autumn
Eighty One
E.S.P.
Everything Happens To Me
Feel Like Makin' Love
Footprints
Four
Four On Six
Gee Baby Ain't I Good
To You
Gone With The Wind
Here's That Rainy Day
I Love Lucy
I Mean You
I Should Care
I Thought About You
If I Were A Bell
Imagination
The Island
Jersey Bounce
Joshua
Lady Bird
Like Someone In Love
Little Sunflower
Lush Life
Mercy, Mercy, Mercy
The Midnight Sun
Monk's Mood
Moonlight In Vermont
My Shining Hour
Nature Boy
Nefertiti
Nothing Personal
Oleo
Once I Loved
Out Of This World
Pent Up House
Portrait Of Tracy
Put It Where You Want It
Robbin's Nest
Ruby, My Dear
Satin Doll
Search For Peace
Shaker Song
Skylark
A Sleepin' Bee
Solar
Speak No Evil
St. Thomas
Street Life
Tenderly
These Foolish Things
This Masquerade
Three Views Of A Secret
Waltz For Debby
Willow Weep For Me
And Many More!

The New Real Book Play-Along CDs (For Volume 1)

CD #1 - Jazz Classics - Lady Bird, Bouncin' With Bud, Up Jumped Spring, Monk's Mood, Doors, Very Early, Eighty One, Voyage **& More!**

CD #2 - Choice Standards - Beautiful Love, Darn That Dream, Moonlight In Vermont, Trieste, My Shining Hour, I Should Care **& More!**

CD #3 - Pop-Fusion - Morning Dance, Nothing Personal, La Samba, Hideaway, This Masquerade, Three Views Of A Secret, Rio **& More!**

World-Class Rhythm Sections, featuring Mark Levine, Larry Dunlap, Sky Evergreen, Bob Magnusson, Keith Jones, Vince Lateano & Tom Hayashi

The New Real Book - Volume 2 (C, Bb or Eb)

Afro-Centric
After You've Gone
Along Came Betty
Bessie's Blues
Black Coffee
Blues For Alice
Body And Soul
Bolivia
The Boy Next Door
Bye Bye Blackbird
Cherokee
A Child Is Born
Cold Duck Time
Day By Day
Django
Equinox
Exactly Like You
Falling Grace
Five Hundred Miles High
Freedom Jazz Dance
Giant Steps
Harlem Nocturne
Hi-Fly
Honeysuckle Rose
I Hadn't Anyone 'Til You
I'll Be Around
I'll Get By
Ill Wind
I'm Glad There Is You
Impressions
In Your Own Sweet Way
It's The Talk Of The Town
Jordu
Killer Joe
Lullaby Of The Leaves
Manha De Carneval
The Masquerade Is Over
Memories Of You
Moment's Notice
Mood Indigo
My Ship
Naima
Nica's Dream
Once In A While
Perdido
Rosetta
Sea Journey
Senor Blues
September Song
Seven Steps To Heaven
Silver's Serenade
So Many Stars
Some Other Blues
Song For My Father
Sophisticated Lady
Spain
Stablemates
Stardust
Sweet And Lovely
That's All
There Is No Greater Love
'Til There Was You
Time Remembered
Turn Out The Stars
Unforgettable
While We're Young
Whisper Not
Will You Still Be Mine?
You're Everything
And Many More!

The New Real Book - Volume 3 (C, Bb, Eb or Bass clef)

Actual Proof
Ain't That Peculair
Almost Like Being In Love
Another Star
Autumn Serenade
Bird Of Beauty
Black Nile
Blue Moon
Butterfly
Caravan
Ceora
Close Your Eyes
Creepin'
Day Dream
Dolphin Dance
Don't Be That Way
Don't Blame Me
Emily
Everything I Have Is Yours
For All We Know
Freedomland
The Gentle Rain
Get Ready
A Ghost Of A Chance
Heat Wave
How Sweet It Is
I Fall In Love Too Easily
I Got It Bad
I Hear A Rhapsody
If You Could See Me Now
In A Mellow Tone
In A Sentimental Mood
Inner Urge
Invitation
The Jitterbug Waltz
Just Friends
Just You, Just Me
Knock On Wood
The Lamp Is Low
Laura
Let's Stay Together
Lonely Woman
Maiden Voyage
Moon And Sand
Moonglow
My Girl
On Green Dolphin Street
Over The Rainbow
Prelude To A Kiss
Respect
Ruby
The Second Time Around
Serenata
The Shadow Of Your Smile
So Near, So Far
Solitude
Speak Like A Child
Spring Is Here
Stairway To The Stars
Star Eyes
Stars Fell On Alabama
Stompin' At The Savoy
Sweet Lorraine
Taking A Chance On Love
This Is New
Too High
(Used To Be A) Cha Cha
When Lights Are Low
You Must Believe In Spring
And Many More!

The All Jazz Real Book

Over 540 pages of tunes as recorded by: Miles, Trane, Bill Evans, Cannonball, Scofield, Brecker, Yellowjackets, Bird, Mulgrew Miller, Kenny Werner, MJQ, McCoy Tyner, Kurt Elling, Brad Mehldau, Don Grolnick, Kenny Garrett, Patitucci, Jerry Bergonzi, Stanley Clarke, Tom Harrell, Herbie Hancock, Horace Silver, Stan Getz, Sonny Rollins, and MORE!

Includes a free CD of many of the melodies (featuring Bob Sheppard & Friends.). $44 list price. Available in C, Bb, Eb

The European Real Book

An amazing collection of some of the greatest jazz compositions ever recorded! Available in C, Bb and Eb. $40

- Over 100 of Europe's best jazz writers.
- 100% accurate, composer-approved charts.
- 400 pages of fresh, exciting sounds from virtually every country in Europe.
- Sher Music's superior legibility and signature calligraphy makes reading the music easy.

Listen to FREE MP3 FILES of many of the songs at **www.shermusic.com!**

See **www.shermusic.com** for more information, including a complete list of tunes in all our fake books.

To order, call (800) 444-7437 or fax (707) 763-2038